Norse Mythology

Ancient Nordic Tales, Gods, Legends, and Beings from A-Z

By History Activist Readers

Introduction

Interested in Norse mythology?

This book is the perfect introduction to the fascinating world of Norse mythology. It contains all the ancient gods, myths, legends, and folklore that have been passed down through oral tradition for centuries.

Norse mythology is a fascinating subject. It tells the ancient stories from the Nordic countries. These tales are filled with magic and adventure, and they provide a unique insight into the beliefs and values of the people who created them.

The Norse pantheon includes such well-known figures as Odin, Thor, and Loki. The body of knowledge known as Norse mythology consists of numerous texts and poems, many of which are fragmentary and date to the medieval period.

Norse gods often use magic to accomplish their goals and can travel to other realms, such as Midgard (the world of humans) and Asgard (the home of the gods). The gods are often engaged in conflicts with each other, as well as with giants, dwarves, and monsters.

Mortal heroes also play a significant role in these Norse stories, testing their strength and courage against seemingly insurmountable odds. In addition to providing entertainment, these stories served an important function in ancient Norse society by helping people to understand their place in the world and teaching them valuable lessons about ethics and morality.

With its rich and colorful history, Norse mythology has inspired artists and writers for generations. Now you can discover this captivating world for yourself with our book.

Table of Content

INTRODUCTION 2
TABLE OF CONTENT 3
NORSE MYTHOLOGY 6
Aesir 7
Asgard 10
Audhumia 13
Álfheimr 14
Balder 15
Bifröst 17
Bor 18
Bragi 19
Brynhild 23
Brísingamen 25
Buri 26
Draugr 27
Draupnir 28
Eitr 29
Elivágar 30
Fenrir 31
Fimbulwinter 33
Folkvangr 35
Forseti 36
Frey 38
Freya 42
Frigg 46
Fyrisvellir 50
Garmr 51
Gerd 52
Ginnungagap 54
Gjallarhorn 56
Gullinbursti 57
Gungnir 58
Heimdall 59
Hell 61
Hell (location) 63
Hermod 65
Hlidskjalf 66
Hod 67

Hoenir 69

Hringhorni 70

Huginn and Muninn 71

Hvergelmir 72

Idunn 73

Jörmungandr 75

Jötun 76

Jötunheimr 81

Loki 84

Midgard 88

Muspelheim 90

Naglfar 91

Nanna 92

Niflheim 93

Njord 94

Norns 97

Náströnd 99

Odin 100

Ragnarok 109

Ratatoskr 116

Sif 117

Sigi 118

Sigyn 119

Sleipnir 120

Sol and Mani 121

Surtr 123

Svartalfer 124

Svaðilfari 125

Tanngrisnir and Tanngnjóstr 126

Thor 127

Thor's Mjolnir 129

Tyr 131

Tyrfing 134

Ull 136

Útgarðar 138

Valhalla 139

Vali 141

Valkyries 142

Vanaheimr 143

Vanir 144

Vidar 147

Vili & Ve **149**
Yggdrasil **151**

Norse Mythology

Aesir

The principal race of gods, led by Odin

The Æsir (Old Norse: Æsir) are the followers of Odin. According to Snorri Sturluson, the main, medieval interpreter of the myths, Aesir means "people of Asia. They are opposed to the Wanen, who are seen primarily as fertility gods. Both of these families of gods arose after Odin, Vili and Ve created the world. Odin was not yet satisfied, but his brothers were, who wanted to go around their creation. Thus the two families of gods were created.

Asia

'[The land] east of the Tanakvísl (Don) in Asia was known as Ásaland [land of the aesir] or Ása-heimr [world of the aesir], and the main fortress in the land they called Ásgard.' (beginning chapter two of Snorri's *Ynglinga saga*)

Etymology

Aesir is plural, *áss* is singular, ásynjur are the feminine aesir, *asynja* is a feminine áss. Etymologically, *áss* seems to be derived from the Indo-European root, which means "breath" and can be associated with life and life-giving forces. A divergent etymology associates the word with kingship

7

and "binding gods," parallel to the terms *bönd* and *höpt*. It also resembles the Old English *os* (god, deity) and *anses* (demigods).

Æsir and Elven

The aesir are referred to as a group in the *Thrymskvida*, among others. They are often mentioned in a formula at the same time as the álfar (elves), as in *Völuspa* (stanza 48): 'How about the aesir,/how about the elves?' Such formulas also occur in *Grímnismál*, *Skírnismál* and *LokÆsirna*.

Ása-Thor

Thor is also Ása-Thor (Thor of the aesir). He is the only god whose name is extended in this way and it is thought that this is why he was considered the best of the aesir.

Cause of war

Later, but "at the beginning of time," there would be quarrels between the two families, partly because the Æsir wanted to build a wall to protect Asgard. The Æsir did not want this because it would hinder their free passage (for the Æsir moved around, they did not stay in one place). Thus a war ensued between the Æsir and the Wanen. The war is known from *Völuspa* and from Snorri's *Ynglinga saga* in his *Heimskringla* and the *Skáldskaparmál* of his *Edda*.

According to the *Völuspa* (stanza 21-24), when she came to them, the aesir are said to have pierced Gullveig (gold-drinking or gold-poisoning, gold-redemption) with burning spears and burned her in the "hall of Hár. Three times she was burned, three times she was reborn. Called Heid (possibly "radiant"), she was a seer and sorceress who worked with *seid* (art of prophecy, magic) and was always "the delight of every wicked woman. The holiest gods had to decide whether for this only the aesir should be punished or all the gods should pay.

Odin threw his spear into the army of his opponents (the *vanir*) and the protective wall of Asgard, the fortress of the aesir, was broken. The vanir were also skilled in warfare.

Reconciliation

Later, the two families would reconcile and create Kvasir to help them keep the peace by acting as a mediator between the two families. Kvasir was the result of the saliva of the aesir and of the vanir, mixed in a cauldron. From Kvasir came the "mead of poetry," from which the *skalden* (poets) would later drink (hence possibly kvas).

In addition, the two families would exchange "hostages. Some of the Æsir would go to live with the Wanen and vice versa. For example, Njord with his daughter Freya and son Freyr would move to the Asgard, and Honir and Mimir, among others, went traveling with the Wanen. Because Honir was incapable of leadership without consulting Mimir, Mirmir was beheaded and sent back to the aesir. Odin managed to keep Mimir's head and it told him of many secret matters. Freya taught the aesir first in the art of *seid*.

Twelve Æsir

Twelve major Aesir are: Odin, Thor, Baldr, Tyr, Bragi, Heimdall, Hod, Vidar, Vali, Ull, Forseti and Loki.

Asgard

The dwelling place of the Aesir gods

Asgaard (Old Norse **Ásgarðr**), in Norse mythology, is the place where the Æsir and Asinnen (the gods) lived, considered separate from the world where humans live (Midgaard), and situated either in space or at the center of the world. Only the worldly Yggdrasil pervades all the spheres (worlds) in the Nordic cosmogony, thus connecting them in the depths of the cosmos.

Asgaard was surrounded by an insurmountable wall, built by a giant, after the war with the Wanen. See also Svadilfari.

The only connection between Midgaard and Asgaard is via the Bifröst Bridge, a rainbow bridge guarded by Heimdall.

Origin and function

Asgaard, according to Northern European mythology, was built by Odin and his brothers with the help of some Thursen. This was after the primeval world in the Ginnungagap had formed by the action of fire and ice and after most of the primeval giants had perished by sacrificing that primeval world (Ymir).

The center of Asgaard is the Iðavöllr field. There in that center Odin (or Wodan) had a palace Gladsheimr built with a throne for himself Hlidskjalf, from which he can look out on all nine worlds, and twelve more thrones for

Æsir whom he designated to rule with him. For the Asinnen there was built the palace Vingólf and later for the heroes also Valhalla.

These are the places where the Gods held meetings about important things. They also met daily at the Well of Urd at the bottom of the root of the world tree Yggdrasil to drink the drink of wisdom.

The stone giant Hrimthur built the wall with the prospect of possessing Freya as his wife as well as the Sun and Moon as a reward. On Loki's cunning advice, the Æsir made an agreement with him that the entire construction would be completed in barely six months, something they considered impossibly feasible. Hrimthur accepted the stipulations, provided he was also allowed to use his horse Svadilfari.
 Much to the Æsir's dismay, Hrimthur seemed likely to succeed in getting the work completed within the allotted time, for barely three days before the final deadline, only a gate arch was missing. Then Loki turned himself into a mare and seduced the stallion Svadilfari who disappeared with the mare for a while. (The mare then gave birth to Odin's stallion Sleipnir). So the giant could not fulfill his contract and, furious with rage, had himself recognized as a giant, after which Thor crushed him with his magic hammer.

Asgard is a giant fortress, a kind of celestial kingdom, with as its main component the twelve palaces of the gods of which Grímnismál speaks. Those twelve heavenly castles are said to be made of gold and precious stones, the vaults of golden spears. Walls and floors covered with gold, and on the roofs shining shields of heroes instead of sun and moon. Thor's dwelling, Thrudheim, is not counted among the heavenly castles, for it is too close to the earthly world and marks the boundary between Asgard and Midgard.

The Twelve Palaces and their *owners*

The order here is purely alphabetical:

1. Alfheim, ("*Alfenheim*") Freyrs Palace
2. Breidablik, ("*Breedglans*") Baldrs Palace
3. Folkvangr, ("*People's Square*") Freyja's Palace with Hall Sessrumnir
4. Gladsheimr, ("*World of Joy*") Odin's Palace with Hall Valhalla
5. Glitnir, ("*Glitter*," *Radiant*) Forseti's Palace
6. Himinbjörg, Heimdalls Palace
7. Nóatún, ("*Ship's Place*") Njörðrs Palace

8.   Sökkvabekkr, ("*Deep Creek*") Saga's Palace
9.   Þrymheimr, Skaði's Palace
10. Valaskjálf, Vali's Palace with Odin's throne Hlidskjalf
11. Vidi, Vidar's Palace, also Landwidi ("*Land width*")
12. Ydalir, Ullrs Palace

Audhumia

Also spelled Audhambla, or Audhumla.

The cow that created Buri by licking ice

Auðumbla (also called Audhumbla, Audumla or Audhumla) was the primordial cow in Nordic mythology.

Audhumla was formed from the melting ice released when the ice of Niflheim and the fire of Muspelheim came together in the Ginnungagap, the primordial void. From those drops of the melted ice, in the beginning of time, Ymir the primal giant had also emerged.Ymir drank from the four streams of milk that flowed from her udders, while feeding herself with the salty of the ripe stones.By licking at the salty ice, she then freed the giant Buri, the primal father of the gods, in three days. Buri's son was Borr, the father of Odin, Vili and Ve. The three brothers created the world by sacrificing Ymir.

Álfheimr

In Nordic mythology, **Alfheim** (or in Old Norse **Álfheimr**, meaning elf-home) is one of the nine worlds surrounding Yggdrasil.

It is on the second highest level in the tree of life Yggdrasil , as is Musspelheim (home of the fire giants). The only world higher is the Asgard, home of the ashes.

Alfheim is inhabited by the *light elves* and by the god Freyr who rules this world.... He had once received Alfheim as a dental gift and has a large and powerful palace standing there. Little else is known about Alfheim, as this world does not appear in many stories.... Alves do not have a prominent role in Nordic mythology, but they do in many other cultures such as Celtic and medieval sagas and legends.

Balder

God of beauty, love, purity, peace, righteousness

Baldr or **Balder** is an Æsir god from Nordic mythology. He was nicknamed the Beautiful and the Good.

Baldr is the son was of the chief god Odin and his wife the goddess Frigg, and lived in the palace Breidablik together with his wife Nanna. As long as he lived, the palace he lived in would spread light over the earth. Therefore, Baldr was also honored as a god of light and spring, of wisdom and eloquence. His justice and good humor made everyone forget gloomy times.

In a dream, it was prophesied that someone would kill Baldr. Therefore, Frigg made everyone take an oath not to harm him. Both trees and animals had to take the oath; no one was forgotten. Because of this measure, everyone soon forgot about the death threat and peace returned. But Loki, the troublemaker, was not satisfied. He learned that the mistletoe had not taken the oath and could therefore kill Baldr. He turned the mistletoe into an arrow and had Hodr, a blind brother of Baldr, fire it at Baldr. Thus, the unsuspecting Hodr killed his own brother.

Baldr cannot go to Valhöll because he did not die honorably on the battlefield, so he must go to Hel (Folkvangr, the "ordinary" underworld). Frigg begs everything in the world to let Baldr come back to the world again so that he can then go to Valhöll. Hel's condition is that then everyone, without exception, must grieve on earth. However, there is a giant who refuses to grieve; this is a disguise of Loki.

At Baldr's burning, his wife Nanna jumps on the fire, killing her and going with Baldr to Hel. When the new world will arise, Baldr will be the main being, after the Ragnarok.

Baldr is also the one whom the giant daughter Skadi had hoped to be allowed to choose from the Æsir in compensation for her father's death. She was only allowed to see the feet of the candidates and chose from them the whitest feet. These, however, were those of the sea god Njord.

Cult

According to James Frazer (author of *The Golden Bough* (1890-1922), a highly influential and controversial work on myths and customs among many peoples), there was a cult of Baldr: a palisade surrounding a sacred place with a temple of sorts, with effigies of gods. The Baldr story lends itself to performance, as do the Greek tragedies.

There were rituals involving fire festivals and human sacrifice. Baldr's funeral, in which a giantess sent a ship into the sea as a funeral pyre, became a midsummer night symbol.

Baldr is also the god of trees: sacred forests in Norway were dedicated to him. The mistletoe (a witch's herb), the wood with which he was killed, rarely grows on an oak tree. Hence the interpretation as a sign of lightning from the gods, sacralizing the oak. The druids among the Celts cut this mistletoe during midsummer with a golden sickle. Fraser sees relics in the St. John's fire. The Germanic people then had the commemoration of Baldr's death.

Bifröst

In Nordic mythology, **Bifröst** (*Rocking Sky Road*) is the tricolored rainbow bridge that connects Asgard and Midgard. It is guarded by the ever-vigilant Heimdal, who keeps an eye on the bridge from his castle Himinbjörg.

It is a flaming bridge, which will collapse on the day of the Ragnarok: it will collapse under the weight of the sons of Surt. All the gods enter this bridge daily on horseback, except Thor, who must walk because he had squandered his own. Thus, each time he has to extinguish his feet in the two rivers that spring from the source of Urd, on which the Norns live and the world tree Yggdrasil stands.

Bor

Also spelled Bur.

The son of Búri, architect of Asgard

Bor(r), in Nordic mythology, is the son of Búri. He married Bestla, the daughter of the giant Bölthorn. They had three sons: Odin, Vili and Vé.

Bragi

God of knowledge, poetry, eloquence, and the patron of skalds

Bragi is the poet god of Nordic mythology. He is the son of Odin and Gunnlod.

When Odin said goodbye to Gunnlod, he still had drops of the poet's forge on his lips. These few drops were enough to completely permeate the child that was already growing in Gunnlod's belly by then (after making love to the disguised Odin for 3 full days).

Etymological origins

Bragi is commonly associated with *bragr* Old Norse for "*poetry*," but also for "*first in charge*," "*leader*." It may be that the god's name is due to this, but it may also be the other way around, that *bragr* means *what Bragi does*.

Edda literature references

Gylfaginning

Snorri Sturluson writes in the *Gylfaginning* after describing Odin, Thor, and Baldr:

One is called Bragi: he is known for wisdom, and above all for fluent speech and dexterity with the word. He knows most about skaldship, and after him skaldship is called *bragr*, and after his name is called the one *bragr man* or woman, who possesses eloquence above all others of women or men. His wife is Iðunn.

Skáldskaparmál

In his *Skáldskaparmál,* Snorri writes:

How can one describe Bragi? By calling him "husband of Iðunn," "first poet," and "the long-bearded god" (after his name a man with big beard is called Baard-Bragi), and "son of Odin

Only here is it clearly stated that Bragi is Odin's son. He also appears in some versions of a list of Odin's sons. But "wish son" in stanza 16 of the LokÆsirna could mean "Odin's son" and is translated by Hollander as "Odin's relative. Bragi's mother is not mentioned in it. If it is Frigg, Frigg acts somewhat dismissive about it in the LokÆsirna in stanza 27 where she complains that if she had a son in Ægirs hall as brave as Baldr Loki would have to fight for his life.

The first part of Skáldskaparmál contains a dialogue between the god giant Ægir and Bragi about the nature of poetry, especially skaldic poetry. Bragi talks about the origin of the poet's mead from the blood of Kvasir and how Odin came to possess it. He then discusses various poetic metaphors known as *kennings*.

In the same poem, however, it is Bragi who initially stops Loki from entering the hall where the festival of the gods is taking place, but this is overruled by Odin. Loki then salutes all the gods and goddesses in the hall except Bragi. Bragi generously offers his sword, horse and an arm ring as gifts of peace, but Loki responds by accusing Bragi of cowardice and says that he would be the most afraid to fight with any of the Æsir and Elves in the hall. Bragi replies, that if they found themselves outside this hall, which is a sanctuary, he would get Loki's head, but Loki agonizingly repeats the accusation. When then Iðunn attempts to appease Bragi, Loki proceeds to accuse her of having embraced her brother's murderer, a matter that has not made it into tradition until our time. Possibly Bragi had knocked Iðunn's brother down or it refers to something entirely different.

Sigrdrífumál

A passage in the Edda poem *Sigrdrífumál* describes how runes are engraved on the sun, the ears of sun lichens and the hooves of others, the teeth of Sleipnir, bear's claws, eagle's jaws, wolf's claws, and many other things including Bragi's tongue. These runes are then shaved off and sent to the outside world mixed with mead so that the Æsir get some of it, the Elves get some of it, and the Humans get some of it. These are then beech runes and birth runes, beer runes and magic runes. The meaning of all this is obscure.

Eiríksmál

In the *Eiríksmál* epic, Odin hears of the arrival in Valhalla of the king of Norway Eirik Bloodaxe and his army. He asks the heroes Sigmund and Sinfjötli to rise to greet him. There Bragi is also mentioned, asking how Odin knows that it is Eirik who is coming and also why Odin has allowed such a king to die.And in the heroic poem *Hákonarmál,* it is Hákon the Good who is taken to Valhalla by the walkure Göndul and Odin sends Hermóðr and Bragi to greet him. In these poems, Bragi can be either a god or a dead hero in Valhalla. It is difficult to make out especially since *Hermóðr* also seems to be sometimes the name of the god and sometimes that of a hero. It may be a parallel to the passage from the LokÆsirna where it is also Bragi who speaks first to Loki when he tries to enter the hall.It may have been the custom that eloquent people skilled in skaldic art also did the welcoming speech to those who entered a hall, just as it was also a Germanic custom to raise a toast to someone.

Identification with Odin himself

According to French professor of languages and Scandinavian civilization at the Sorbonne Régis Boyer, the figure of Bragi could well be an alias of Odin himself, since both are at the basis of poetry. (Régis Boyer, *Héros et dieux du Nord : guide iconographique*, Paris, Flammarion, 1997. 185 p. Tout l'art. Encyclopedia. ISBN 2080122746). As is often the case in polytheistic systems, one god is present in many aspects in the form of other gods. This also makes precisely the immense richness of polytheism in facets, nuances and concepts.

Bragi Boddason

Snorri Sturluson clearly distinguishes between the mortal skald Bragi Boddason and the god Bragi. The appearance of Bragi in the *LokÆsirna* suggests that even if the two were originally the same, they have become distinct from each other even for this author, or that the chronology has been very mixed up and Bragi Boddason has also been relegated to mythological time. Legendary chronology gets confused quite often. In the 19th century, the question of whether Bragi first appeared as a god or as a deified edition of the poet Bragi Boddason was widely debated. Especially the German scholars Eugen Mogk and Sophus Bugge participated in this. The debate remained undecided.

Brynhild

A female warrior, one of the Valkyries, and daughter of Odin

Brünnhilde (also called Brynhildr, Brunhild or Brynhild) is a shield maiden and a Walkure in Germanic mythology. Brynja means chain mail in Icelandic. Brünnhilde appears in the Völsunga saga and some Edda poems, among others. She also appears in the *Nibelungen song* and in Richard Wagner's opera *Der Ring des Nibelungen*.

In the Sigrdrífumál, "the song of Sigrdrifa," Sigurd and Sigrdrifa, Brünnhilde in the "supernatural" guise of walkure, meet for the first time. Sigurd frees her from her sleep. Odin had stabbed Sigrdrifa with the sleep thorn because she felled Gunnar with the Helm, Agnar's opponent, while Odin had granted him victory. Sigurd frees her from the coat of mail, which seems to have fused with her flesh, after which she awakens. They swear each other allegiance and promise to marry each other. Sigurd gives her the ring of the dwarf Andvari, which has a curse on it without Sigurd's knowledge. During this first meeting, their daughter Aslaug must have been conceived. Later at Heimir's court, they see each other again. Heimir has married Brünnhild's sister Bekkhild and is Brünnhild's foster father.

23

Budli is her father and Atli her brother. They belong, according to the Skaldskaparmal, to the Budlingen, a dynasty that has (an earlier) Budli as its progenitor. Budli is the son of Halfdan the Elder.

Brísingamen

Brinsingamen, in Nordic mythology, was a necklace made by dwarves.

Freya, who loved beauty, had to have this necklace at any cost. To get her, she slept with the four (hideous) dwarves who made the necklace. The Brinsingamen was her most precious possession.

Buri

God of gods

In Nordic mythology, **Búri** is the second primal giant (next to Ymir). Buri is licked out of the original stagnant ice mass by the primordial cow Audhumbla. Búri is the primordial father both of all giants and gods (Æsir and Wanen).

From him the first descended Borr (or *Bor*) and Bestla from whom the precursors of the Æsir (Odin) and Wanen (Vili) as well as Ve.

The following lines can be read in the Gylfaginning of Snorri Sturluson's Prose-Edda:

Búri is not mentioned anywhere in the Poetic Edda, and only once in the skaldic corpus. In *Skáldskaparmál*, Snorri Sturluson quotes the following verse from the 12th-century skald Þórvaldr blönduskáld.

Draugr

The **draugen** (Old Norse: *draugr*, Icelandic: *dragur*, Faroese: *dreygur*, Norse, Swedish, and Danish: *draugen*) is an undead creature from Nordic mythology that haunts around its grave and usually protects a treasure.The word comes from Proto-Indo-European *droughos, "ghost," from the root *dreugh-, "to deceive"; compare the Dutch *gedrocht*.

Features

According to old legends, he is so black that it hurts your eyes. The four white eyes have no pupils. The draugen is omniscient.

Legend

Several people tried to tame the dragons, but each was found with no memory.

Draupnir

Draupnir is a golden arm ring owned by Odin, the highest Ase in Nordic mythology. This ring was a source of endless wealth, for every ninth morning he secreted eight new gold rings, just like himself.

Draupnir was forged by the dwarven brothers Brokkr and Eitri (or Sindri). The name means *Dripper*. This ring was made by the dwarves as one of three special gifts for the gods, which also included Mjollnir the hammer of Thor and Gullinbursti the golden ever of Freyr.

The reason for making them was a bet that went out from Loki to challenge them to do so. When Loki then lost the bet, because the dwarves had succeeded in making the works of art, the latter was unable to keep his promise to the Sons of Ivaldi (he had wagered his head) and was punished for it: his lips were joined with wire.

The ring was placed on the pyre by Odin at the corpse burning of his murdered son Baldr.

The ring was then withdrawn by Hermóðr. It was offered as a gift to Gerd by Freyr's servant Skirnir when the fertility god courted her as described in the Eddal song *Skírnismál*.

Draupnir is also the name of a dwarf named in the *Völuspá*.

Eitr

Eitr is a fictional substance in Nordic mythology. This liquid substance is the origin of all living entities. The first giant Ymir was created from eitr. The substance is considered highly toxic as it is also produced by Jörmungandr (the Midgard serpent) and other serpents.

Etymology and meaning

The word **eitr** exists in most Nordic languages (all derived from Old Norse) in Danish *edder*, in Swedish *etter*, in German *Eiter* (lett. *etter*),in Old Saxon *ĕttar*, in Old English ăttor and in Dutch *ether*. The meaning of the word is very broad: *volatile, poisonous, evil, bad, furious, sinister,* etc.

In common Scandinavian folklore, it is used as a synonym for snake venom. The last line of the stanza in Vafþrúðnismál where Vafþrúðnir says, "that is why we so easily become enraged," is a play on words with the meaning of the word *eitr*, as it also means *anger/rage* (as in "*poisoning a relationship*").

Elivágar

In Nordic mythology, in Niflheim there was a spring, Hvergelmir or the Rushing Cauldron. From this spring flowed eleven streams, they bore the collective name **Elivágar** (storm waves), and individually they were called Svöl, Gunurd (Gunnthra), F(j)orm, Fimbul(thul, Þul), Slíd, Hríd, Sylg, Ylg, Víd, Leiptr and Gjöll, with Gjöll close to the lowest point, Niflhel (dark hell).

When the poisonous rivers flowed far from their source, they turned into ice and layer upon layer of ice grew within Ginnungagap. To the north was the ice of Niflheim (dark world) and to the south was the fire of Muspellsheim. Where frost and heat came together, drops formed and life began through the power of heat. In this the figure of the primal giant Ymir appeared.

Fenrir

Fenrir (or **Fenrisulfr** or **Fenries**) is the (middle) son of the God of Deception Loki and the female frost giant Angrboda. He is the brother of Hel, the goddess of the underworld and Midgardsorm, the Midgaard snake. Fenrir was neither man nor god, but resembled a small dog when he was young and Odin took him to the Asgaard where the æsen, Odin's followers, lived. All prophecies said Fenrir would become a problem for the æsen.

He developed into a giant wolf with terrible jaws and was reputed to be evil. Moreover, not only was he strong, he had also inherited Loki's cunning. Eventually he dared to threaten even the æsen.

At some point he had become so unmanageable that the gods among themselves devised a plan to bind him. First an attempt was made with the chain *Lœðing*, but it broke. Then a chain twice as strong was fetched, the chain *Drómi*, but it too was too weak.

Finally, Odin sent Freyr's messenger, Skírnir, to the svartalvene (black elves, also called night elves) to have a special necklace made. This should be so strong that even Fenrir would not be able to break it. It became a very fine necklace, the Gleipnir, which was as slender and soft as a rope made of silk. Gleipnir was made from six ingredients that no one can find today: the breath of fish, the beard of a woman, the saliva of a bird, the roots of the mountain, the sound of a cat's paws and the sinews of a bear.

The æsen trapped Fenrir on the small island of Lyngvi in Lake Ámsvartnir (pitch black). They entered into a wager with him: Fenrir claimed he was so terribly strong that they wanted to see proof of that. They would tie him up and Fenrir would have to break his shackles. If he failed, he was so weak that they need not fear him - and would release him.

Fenrir, however, had little faith in the æsen. He demanded that someone put his hand in his maw, as "collateral." Only Týr, the god of war, dared to do this. Týr placed his right hand in Fenrir's maw, and when the wolf could not break his shackles, he bit off Týr's hand during his attempt to break free. Thus, Týr lost his right hand.

The loose end of Gleipnir, Gelgia, was thrust through a huge rock, Gjoll, which was driven deep into the earth. With the huge rock Thviti, Gjoll was driven even deeper into the earth.

31

Fenrir gasped at the æsen; they put a sword in his maw with the point
raised so that he could not bite. His drooling created the river Ván (hope).

Only at the end of the world, during Ragnarok, will Fenrir break free and
be killed by Odin's son, named Vidar, who will avenge his father.

Fimbulwinter

In Nordic mythology, **Fimbulvetr** (*Dragging Winter*), also *Fimbulwinter*, is the winter that preceded the Great War, the Ragnarok, (the twilight of the gods in Germanic mythology).

Characteristics of Fimbulvetr

In the Poetic Edda Song of Vafþrúðnir, the term is considered synonymous with the downfall of the world.In this winter, all oaths of men would be broken, all family ties would be meaningless, daughters would hate their mothers, the honorable would be fools and the honest would be turned into liars. There are then countless wars and brothers kill brothers.

The Fimbulwinter lasts for three years, and then Heimdal blows the Gjallar horn as the Giants (Thursen and Jötun) break through the protective rampart, as the dead sail away from Nástrond with Naglfar, and the followers of Surt enter the rainbow bridge Bifrost. To everyone, the sound of this horn halts the breath; everyone now knows that the final battle has begun.

Fimbulwinter lasts three consecutive winters where snow comes in from all sides, uninterrupted by a summer.

Original spelling

In Old Norse, the original spelling of the word is **Fimbulvintr** (Denmark and Sweden) or **Fimbulvetr** (Iceland and Norway). The meaning of *fimbul* is *large*, *grand*, so the correct interpretation of the word is "the grand winter."

Meaning

In Sweden and Norway and other Nordic countries, the term **fimbulwinter** is also used on occasion when referring to an extremely severe cold winter with exceptionally large amounts of snow.

There have been some popular speculations as if this mythological concept were related to the climate change that occurred in the Nordic lands at the end of the Nordic Bronze Age, around 650 BCE. Before that climate change, the Nordic lands were noticeably warmer.

But this is a mythological concept that may have been represented in this "local" form, but refers to a much broader cosmic event, comparable to the Indian concept of Kali Yuga or to what in our cosmology is now referred to as the final crack.

Folkvangr

A field ruled over by the goddess Freyja

In Nordic mythology, **Folkvangr** (Old Norse for *Folk Square*) was Freya's abode in Asgaard. According to sources, this was an idyllic land where Sessrumnir was also located. Extrapolation from these sources (especially Gylfaginning) implies that love songs were continuously played there. But Freya was also the one who received half the number of those who fell in battle. As a result, there is also a martial connotation to her stay.

Forseti

God of justice

Forseti in mythology is a Nordic god dedicated to justice. It is assumed that the northern cult of the god that in Old Norse **Forseti**.

Under the names *Forseti,* the god plays a role in Nordic mythology as one of the twelve Æsir gods, especially as god of law, peace and truth. There he is the son of Baldur and Nanna. In the sky-god Asgaard, he has a palace or hall Glitnir, which means "shining" and refers to the silver roof and golden pillars that could be seen from a great distance. In Old Norse, the name meant "president," and the word has the meaning of president in modern Icelandic and Faroese.

Forseti was considered the wisest and most eloquent god of Asgaard. Unlike his relative god Týr, who spoke justice over more serious crimes, Forseti negotiated and decided smaller disputes. In his hall he provided justice to anyone who asked him to do so, and it was claimed that his judgment was always seen as fair by all parties. Like his father Baldur, he was a gentle god who advocated peace, and so anyone who followed his judgment could live in safety. Forseti was held in such high esteem that only the most solemn oaths were spoken in his name.

He is not mentioned as a warrior in Ragnarok and it is assumed that he did not participate in martial affairs as a god of peace. A factor may have been that the surviving version of Ragnarok belongs to Nordic mythology.

Frey

God of agriculture, prosperity, life, and fertility

Freyr, also called *Frey, Frø, Fricco Froði* (*Froðr* in Old Norse means *fertile, wise*) and *Yngvi-Freyr*, is the Nordic phallic god of male sexuality. He is twin brother of the goddess *Freya*, a later form of the great goddess *Frigg*.

His name means *lord*, just as Freya's name means *lady*, related to the name of the Indian goddess *Priya*, whose name also means lady. A name of the Hindu goddess of love Lakshmi is "Haripriya" (beloved of Hari).

Etymological origin

Freyr means *Lord* (in Old High German *fro*) and is thus not actually a name, but a title. Possibly it was a taboo name for a god whose actual name is not known to us.

He first appears in chapter 10 of the Ynglingasage, under the name Yngvi from whom the Swedish royal house (the Ynglinge) is said to descend, and in chapter 11 as the father of Fjölnir under the name Yngvi-Freyr. Etymologically, the designation of the Germanic tribe *Ingaevonen* is related. The contraction would then trace back to Old Germanic *Ingwia-fraujaz* (= lord of the Ingaevons).

The town of Forrières in the Belgian Ardennes owes its name to this deity, as does the forest a little further east that is still called *Forêt de Freyr*. In Dinant, a climbing rock is named after him Freÿr, with a trema emphasizing the pronunciation.

Genealogy

Freyr refers to a deity belonging to the Delusions. His father is Njord, whom Freyr fathered in an incestuous relationship with his sister Freya. Later, with the giantess Gerdr, Freyr had a son, Fjölnir, who, according to the saga, became the victorious king of Sweden.

As a dental gift, Freyr was assigned Alfheim, the world of the fertile nature spirits, the Alven.

He has Skírnir, Byggvir and Beyla in permanent service.

Edda

Once Freyr had sat on Odin's throne Hlidskjalf, from which one has a view of all nine worlds. His eye then fell on a wondrously beautiful giant daughter Gerdr in Jötunheim. He sent Skirnir to the giantess.

To get her, according to the Skírnismál, he had to pawn his sword to her father. Thus he lost the wonder sword that was able to strike by itself forever. Therefore, he used a substitute sword made of deer horn with which he could fell many a giant, but which could not serve him to repel the fire giant Surt at the end of time.

Attributes

His best-known attributes are:

- The ship Skíðblaðnir, which the dwarves had made for him. The ship always got a favorable wind in its sails and accommodated all the gods, in full armor. Yet the ship was so artfully made that it could fit small folded up in a bag.

- The golden boar Gullinbursti ("golden bristles"). The boar could run through the air and across the sea faster than a horse, and it could illuminate even the darkest night.
- His self-wielding sword, which he had given to his servant Skirnir when the latter went to visit the giantess Gerðr for him to pair her with Freyr.

In the Nordic world, Freyr is often depicted as a bearded man with distinctly disproportioned virile attributes. According to certain authors, this would therefore be a *phallic* deity, something that was confirmed by archaeological finds. He was often represented simply as a blessing and protective phallus, as is the case with the Indian god Shiva in the form of the lingam.

Function

Peace and fertility seem to have been closely linked in Nordic religion. Offerings with which it was hoped to invoke fertility and peace were often made at the same time, and it was considered one of the fertility gods' special duties to maintain peace among the people. In Freyr's temples, therefore, the carrying of weapons was forbidden, and in his holy places there was a taboo on mutual bloodshed. According to Adam of Bremen, there were celebrations every nine years during which both human and animal sacrifices took place.

Freyr occupied such an important position among the gods that his statue in the great temple at Uppsala stood next to the statues of Odin and Thor.

Cult

Because of his position as the god of fertility, he was especially worshipped by the peasants, who were the largest population group.

According to Snorri Sturluson, both Freyr and his sister Freya were dazzlingly beautiful and unimaginably powerful. As the radiant and generous giver of rain and sunshine and of growth, Freyr was considered the most glorious among the gods.Freyr's cult bore strong resemblance to that of his sister, Freya, who ruled over sexual lust and about whom quite a lot is known. We know that Freyr was widely worshipped, but other than some vague impressions of rituals, knowledge about his cult is lost.

Freyr was associated with horses, which, judging from the legends, were also sacrificed to him. Horses were popular sacrificial animals during the time of the migrations, and their role in Freyr's worship possibly dates back to that time. The importance of the horse cult is evidenced by the bones and hides found in Swedish cult sites. Such finds have also been made in Viking graves, especially in burial vessels.

Sex Rites

Today, researchers generally assume that fertility was an integral part of Viking society, and the most famous find to demonstrate the rites associated with it was a figurine found in Rällinge, Sweden, in the early 20th century.Its appearance indicates that it had to do with fertility rites and it is usually interpreted as the male side of Freya, her twin brother Freyr.Furthermore, Adam van Bremen talks about the phallus symbol, the figurine of Freyr, which stood in the temple of Uppsala and about the rancid chants that were sung during rituals. In *Völsa þáttr* there is an account of the worship of a horse phallus by a pagan family, and that account is related to an ancient Indo-Aryan sacrificial ritual.

In Ibn Fadlan's description of the burial of a Scandinavian chief on the Volga, a slave girl who was to be sacrificed had to undergo several sexual rituals.

Freya

Freya, also spelled Freyia, Freyja, or Frea.

Goddess of fertility, love, beauty, magic, war, and death

Freya, also called **Frea** or **Freyja**, is the Nordic goddess of fertility, love and lust.

Freya was beautiful and powerful (such a woman is called *frova*). At the same time, she was also a fighter. From time to time she competed in some battle or other. When it came down to it, she threw herself into battle with as much fire as a Walkure. This is also the reason why Freya is sometimes considered the ringleader of the Walkures, but that is Odin in whose service they are.

Freya, according to the Germanic people, was the most beautiful of all gods and goddesses.

Attributes

Freya possessed many attributes for a Nordic goddess. The most famous of these is the Brisingamen necklace. A story has been handed down in the Flateyjarbók about how she acquired this piece of jewelry: the makers of this necklace were four dwarves. These dwarves demanded that she spend one night with each of them in exchange for the jewel, to which she agreed. The Flateyjarbók was written in the fourteenth century by two Christian priests. There is therefore reason to doubt whether it is a truthful representation of the stories told in the times before Christianity.

There is also a modern interpretation of this story: this is that each of the dwarves symbolizes one of the four elements. By uniting with the essence of each of these elements, Freya gained wisdom and strength symbolized by Brisingamen.

Another very famous attribute of Freya are her forest cats, which pull her chariot. These animals are almost always seen depicted with Freya. These forest cats, which were considered her pet animals, symbolized the magic of which Freya was also the goddess. One forest cat is black and the other white. Later in the time of the Christians, Freya was enthralled and her forest cats were considered evil forces. That is, only the black forest cat; the white cat was omitted by the Christians. This is also why a black cat is considered magical.

Freya also had another attribute that also symbolized her magic, which was a cloak made of eagle or hawk feathers. With this she could transform herself into a bird at any time. In the Þrýmskviða, she lends this garment to Loki, allowing him, dressed as Freya's servant, to accompany Thor to the giant Thymr.

To the Vikings, the Pleiades were the chickens of Freya (also in other northern European cultures, such as Old English and Old German, this star group is represented as a chicken with chicks).

Kinships

Freya is originally one of the Wans. That is the more earthly family of gods, besides the Æsir, who are atmospheric gods. She is sometimes identified with Odin's wife Frigg (also called Frigga, Frija or Fricka), the Nordic goddess of fertility, who has more or less the same responsibilities. Yet Freya lives in Asgard, the land of the Norse gods of nature and fertility.

Freya is the daughter of the god of navigation Njord. The god Freyr (or Frey) is her twin brother. Although it is also speculated that Freyr is simply the male form of Freya. In Germanic/Nordic mythology, different forms or genders of one deity do occur more often. Think for example of Odin or Loki manifesting in many different forms and genders.

Freya is married to Odr, and with him she has two daughters, Hnossa ("jewel") and Germesie.

Myths

43

Myths also exist about this goddess. For example, Freya played an important role in the well-known myth about the hammer Mjölnir, which was stolen by the giant Þrymr and demanded Freya's hand as ransom. Freya, however, did not want this and so Thor had to retrieve the Mjölnir himself. Thor, disguised as Freya, set out with Loki to meet the giant.

The giant of course realized this, but still Thor was able to retrieve his hammer and then killed the giant.

Aegir then has to brew the mead and Loki behaves improperly at the feast, arguing with many gods and goddesses present. He even mocks Wodan, like a tramp playing with ghosts, as witches and wizards do. Loki insults Frigg and Freya, but he is in awe of Thor. Loki leaves as a salmon, but still tells Aegir that his possessions will go up in flames. The Æsir are later able to capture Loki and tie him up.

There is also a myth about the giant who built the foundations of Asgard. He is said to have demanded the sun, the moon and the hand of Freya as wages. At the time, this trio was seen as uniting the forces of light, love and growth. But because of Loki's cunning, this giant did not get his wall around Asgard finished in time and with it, he did not get his reward. Loki did this by turning himself into a mare (i.e., he could change shape and gender) to distract the horse that carried the giant's belongings. From the intercourse of the mare (Loki) and the horse, according to the myths, came the eight-legged horse of Odin: Sleipnir.

Furthermore, there is another myth that explains the seasons. In fact, Freya was married to Odr (Odhur) who loved traveling very much. One day he left his wife and two children to go traveling. Freya then went looking for Odr and soon autumn arrived and then winter. Eventually Freya finds Odr again under a laurel tree and together they return to Asgard. And during the journey back, it soon becomes spring again.

Freya as a battle goddess

As a battle goddess, Freya rides Hildisvín, the warrior. In *Hyndluljóð,* it is told that she turned *Ottar* into an ever to hide him. The ever has a special relationship with Northern European mythology, both in connection with its fertility and its combativeness. The ever was used as a protective talisman in war, probably because true evers can attack particularly ferociously, (especially females defending their young). Helmets from the 7th century found in Sweden have depictions of warriors wearing large evers as a helmet mark. Also in Beowulf, the ever on the helmet is said to serve to protect the life of the warrior wearing it.

Some of those chosen in battle are called by Freya to her castle Folkvangr, where they have a good life in the afterlife. (For his part, Odin also chooses his own chosen warriors for his Valhalla, according to *Grímnismál*

Freya's association with death is touched upon in Egil's saga, when his daughter Thorgerda (Þorgerðr) threatens suicide after the death of her brother: "I will not eat until I sit with Freya."

Homologues

Freya is considered the Northern European counterpart of Venus and Aphrodite, although she possesses a combination of attributes not present in any mythology of other Indo-European peoples. She is closer in this respect to the Mesopotamian Ishtar, insofar as she is also involved in both love and battle. Some believe that she is the most direct mythological successor to the hermaphrodite fertility god Nerthus.

Friday is named after this goddess, although there is also strong name affinity with Frigg.

Frigg

Also spelled Frigga.

Goddess of love, marriage, fertility, family, civilization, and a prophetess

In Norse mythology, **Frigg** (Edda's) or **Frigga** (*Gesta Danorum*) was called the "First among the goddesses," the wife of Odin, queen of the Æsir, and goddess of the firmament.

Features

As Ásynjur, she is the goddess or patroness of marriage, motherhood, fertility, love and sexuality, housekeeping and the domestic arts. All of these together are characteristic features of a mother goddess.

Her main function, as expressed in the Nordic mythological stories, is that of wife and mother, but she has more. She has the power of prophecy, though she herself does not say what she knows, and she is the only one allowed to sit next to Odin on the lofty throne Hlidskjalf from which one has a full view of the universe. Together with her husband, she participates in the Wild Hunt (Asgardreid).

Frigg discourages Odin from going to Vafthrudnir, see Vafþrúðnismál.

Frigg's children are Baldr, Hodr (and in an English source also Wecta). Her stepchildren are Hermóðr, Heimdall, Týr, Vidar, Váli, and Skjoldr. Thor is either a brother or a stepson of hers. Her faithful companion is Eir, doctor of the Æsir and goddess of healing.

Frigg's companions are Hlín (a patron goddess), Gná (messenger goddess), and Fulla (a fertility goddess). It is not always clear whether these companions are not in fact aspects of herself (cf. avatara).

According to the LokÆsirna poem, Frigg is the daughter of Fjorgyn (male version of "Earth," cf. female Earth version: Thor's mother). Her mother is not known in the stories that have survived.

Etymology

The name Frigg means "love" or "beloved." The word comes from Proto-Germanic *frijjō, cf. Sanskrit priyā "dear woman"). She was known in many cultures from the northern half of Europe, sometimes under slight name variations: for example, **Frea** in southern Germany, **Frija** or **Friia** in Old High German, **Friggja** in Sweden, **Frīg** (genitive Frīge) in Old English, and **Frika** in Wagner's operas. Modern translations often change Frigg to *Frigga*. Woman Hollow (makes snow by knocking out her pillow) and Perchta (controls spinning) are also considered relics of the Frigg concept.

In Faroese (the language of the Faroe Islands), *friggja* means "courting" (as when you want to ask someone to marry you). This again indicates the connection with marriage and marital pleasures. Our word "make love" comes from the same kinship of language and meaning.

Attributes and residence

In Scandinavia, the constellation "Orion" is known as "Frigg's spinning wheel or spinning skirt" (*Friggerock*). Some point out that this constellation is on the celestial equator, so it spins in the night sky. This might have triggered the association with the spinning wheel of the sky goddess. She is said to have woven or spun the mists and clouds, see also Orion Nebula.

The hall space where Frigg resides in Asgaard is Fensalir. This means "Swamp Halls." This may indicate that swampy or muddy land (beginning land) was specially dedicated to her. But nothing definite is known about this. Compare the swamp woman and white wolves.

The goddess Sága, described as drinking with Odin from golden cups in her hall "Sunken Banks," could be Frigg by another name.

Symbols associated with Frigg:

- Keys
- Spider skirts
- Coil
- Mistletoe

The connection between Frigg and Freya

Frigg is the supreme goddess of the Æsir, where Freya is the supreme goddess of the Vanir. There have been quite a few arguments for and against the idea that Frigg and Freya would actually be the same goddess, avatars of each other. Some rely on linguistic analysis, others on the fact that Freya was not known in the south, but rather in the far north. Moreover, in some places they were considered the same goddess, in others different.There are, of course, obvious similarities between the two:

- They both had a cloak of eagle feathers and could change shape
- Frigg was married to Odin
- Freya was married to Óðr
- They each had a special necklace
- Both had a personification of Earth as a parent
- Both were invoked at birth (including labor and labor)

But in certain texts, they sometimes both appear at the same time.

Loki behaves improperly at the feast of Aegir and argues with many gods and goddesses present. He even mocks Wodan, like a tramp playing with ghosts, as witches and wizards do. Loki insults Frigg and Freya, but he is in awe of Thor. Loki leaves as a salmon, but still tells Aegir that his possessions will go up in flames. The Æsir are later able to capture Loki and tie him up.

Another approach is that of an original triad of these two goddesses together with still Hnoss or Iðunn. This triad is then associated with
48

different periods of women's lives. But the spheres of influence of Frigg and Freya do not quite match the spheres of influence often encountered in other goddess triads. This could mean that the evidence is not so conclusive, but it could also mean that something important is eluding us about northern European culture in comparison to the more southern and that of the Celts (see also Frige in that regard).

Finally, there is another line of argument that Frigg and Freya would have been similar goddesses from different pantheons, first merged into a single deity, but where these two goddesses were subsequently separated again. (See also Frige). Such a view is consistent with the theological approach to some Greek, Roman and Egyptian deities of late classical antiquity.

Fyrisvellir

Fyrisvellir was the swampy plain (Vellir) south of Gamla Uppsala where travelers had to leave the ships to continue on foot to the Temple of Uppsala and the Hall of the Swedish King.

The name comes from the Old Norse Fyrva meaning "to ebb away" and referred to the partially flooded marshy plains that today have been drained and where the city of Uppsala is located. In the Middle Ages there was a royal estate called Førisæng or "Fyrisweide" near this area. The small lakes Övre Föret and Nedre Föret are remnants of this swamp and retained a modern form of the word Fyri.

According to Nordic mythology, the battle between Haki and Hugleik, and later that between Haki and Jorund, took place on this plain. It was also the location of the Battle of Fyrisvellir between Erik the Conqueror and his cousin Styrbjörn the Strong in the year 980.

A saga about Hrólf Kraki tells of him throwing gold on this plain when he and his retinue fled from the Swedish king Aðils. The king's retinue gave up pursuit to collect the gold. In Skaldic poetry, gold was often referred to by the kenning "the seed of Fyrisvellir."

Garmr

In Nordic mythology, **Garmr** or Janker was a huge dog that guarded the gateway to Niflheim or Nebula Kingdom in the Rotshol or Gnipahellir. This was normally stained with blood. After Fenrir, Garmr was the largest of the dogs, and during the Ragnarok, Garmr and the war god Týr would kill each other.

In the song *Völuspá,* the line *Geyr Garmr mjök / fyr Gnipahelli* (Fierce bark Janker now / for Rotshol) is repeated three times. The first time refers to the onset of Fimbulvetr. The second entry indicates the breakthrough of the giants into the world of the gods and the third time refers to the beginning of the new world on the plain Vigrid.

Gerd

Fertility goddess, who is associated with the earth

Gerd, **Gärd**, **Gerdhr**, **Gerda**, **Gerdur** or *Gerdr* (Old Norse *Gerðr*) in Nordic mythology is the daughter of the giant Gymir and the giantess Aurboda. Her brother's name is Beli. They lived in Jötunheimr, the world of giants inaccessible to humans.

The most beautiful among all creatures, she was possibly considered the personification of fertility and sex. Her shining naked arms illuminated sky and sea.

One day she became the object of love because of the fertility god Freyr, who was enamored by her and therefore barely functioning. The Eddal song Skírnismál recounts what happened then.

She had never intended to marry Freyr, so she refused his proposals that reached her through Skirnir, even after the latter had brought her eleven golden apples (immortality food of the Æsir) and the ring Draupnir. Only when Skirnir threatened to use Freyr's sword to make the world disappear under a thick sheet of ice did she agree to marry Freyr.

Etymology and symbolism

Her name probably comes from *gerða* meaning to *fence*, related to *garðr*, *gaard* (*enclosed space* such as a garden) (English *yard* and via Danish *garth*).

The union of Gerdr with Freyr bears resemblance to that of the giantess Skaði with the fertility god Njördr. In both cases, this could indicate a way of reconciling the forces of death and darkness with those of Nature's regenerative capacity.

Gerd can thus be considered a deity of fertile soil, similar to Nerthus, but there are also elements pointing to walkure properties. That her dwelling place is demarcated by flames shows that the mother's name Aurboda could also be read as "Örboða," (*coals that give cold*) a typical Walkure name.

Ginnungagap

The **Ginnungagap** (*the abyss of ginn*; Old Norse *ginn, magic, magic,* it corresponds to Sanskrit *tat* meaning *that*) is the chasm of apparent emptiness, matter-free space, nothingness or vacuum from Nordic mythology. The chasm is also subsequently called **Himthusen** but occurs as the original gaping abyss in the creation story of the Edda.

The Ginnungagap was the meeting place between mists and fire at the beginning of time, before the cosmos formed in this void. Because Niflheim (a mist world) and Muspelheim (a fire world) came together in the Ginnungagap at the beginning of time, Ymir was created which was used as material for further creation. Compare: Chaos.

The Prose Edda recounts further

"When the rivers called Elivágar had flowed so far away from their source that the icy cold parts within them began to harden, like molten iron flowing away from the fire, they became ice. And when this ice came to a standstill and flowed no further, the water vapor that rose from the icy mass struck down upon it and froze into hoarfrost; and one layer of hoarfrost deposited itself upon another, all the way to Ginnungagap.'

'The northern part of Ginnungagap was filled by a heavy mass of ice and frost, with rain and freezing wind before it. But in the southern part of Ginnungagap it was lightened by the sparks and glowing embers that came flying in from Muspelheim.'

'As all that came from Niflheim was cold and terrible, so all that lay near Múspell was hot and light. In Ginnungagap itself it was a lee as in windless weather. And when the hot glow covered the frost, it began to melt and drip, and in the cold droplets life arose by the power of the one who sent the heat, and it took the form of a man. That man is called Ýmir, but the riding giants call him Aurgelmir. From him the riding giants are descended as is said in the Völuspá.

The cradle of emergence

Ginnungagap, then, is the gaping void in which worlds spontaneously condense and form from nothingness. There is separation or polarization from that neutral nothingness into the warm light, and the cold dark. The primordial flow of swirling particles that seem to bubble up from nothingness thereby differentiates and transforms into successive more solid forms of energy and matter in successive worlds.

Etymological name origin

The root word *ginn* means *magic, magic*. The derivative *ginnung* is *enchantment* and the Vans are called *ginnregin* or *magical powers*. So the primordial space was full of powers that did not yet have a divine order.

Ginn, by the way, is a word that is more common especially in religious or spiritual language. *Ginnheiligar* would mean as much as *with holy power*. Already in the language of runic monuments (Stentoften and Björkertorp) ginna- or ginnurunar (power runes) are mentioned. Dr. Jan de Vries (linguist) states that if one considers that in addition to this the word *gandr* is also in ablaut as *magic*, one may assume to be in a magical sphere here and that the word *ginnungagap* is the communication of *a primeval space filled with magical power*.

Gjallarhorn

The **Gjallar horn** is a horn from Nordic mythology. It is kept by Heimdal, the guardian of the gods, who guards the rainbow bridge Bifrost and is hidden under the Yggdrasil tree. Through this horn, he transmits messages from the gods from Asgard to the mortals in Midgard.

With Ragnarok, Heimdal makes this horn resound loudly everywhere, so that all the gods and their followers know that the decisive battle has arrived and that they must make their way to the Vigrid Plain, the plain where the battle between good and evil will be fought. But in Nordic mythology, this is not a battle between good and evil as in the Christian sense. Rather, it is a battle between chaos and cosmos.

From the Gjallar horn, according to Snorri Sturluson in anticipation Mímir, the mead of wisdom drinks from the bottom of its spring.

Gullinbursti

Gullinbursti means *golden bristles* and is the boar of the god Freyr.
Another name is Slíðrugtanni (*dangerous tusks*). It is one of the many
creations of the dwarves (namely of the dwarf Brokkr). The animal pulls
Freyr's chariot through water and through air and often illuminates the
night with its golden bristles. One then sees for a long time only the lower
rows of spines, as a sign that the giant creature is passing through the
dark skies.

The manufacture of Gullinbursti is recounted in the Skáldskaparmál, part
of the prose Edda.

When Loki had made the four sons of Ivaldi Sif's golden hair, Freyr's ship
Skíðblaðnir and Odin's spear Gungnir, he wagered his head on Brokkr that
the latter's brother Eitri would not be able to make anything so valuable.
To accomplish gifts for Freyr, Eitri then threw a pigskin into the stove while
Brokkr operated the bellows, and together they made the ever Gullinbursti
with its golden mane and bristles that glowed in the darkness and threw off
gensters.

Incidentally, the shrewd Loki retained his head, because as he pretended,
otherwise his neck would be damaged, and it was not included in the bet.

The first Swedish kings, the (Ynglinge), wore helmets with the image of a
boar. One of them was called Hidisvin, which was Freya's boar. The boar
helmet is also mentioned in the Anglo-Saxon poem Beowulf. Another royal
heirloom was the Sviagriss, a ring with the image of a piglet.

The wild boar is also a somewhat common theme in other mythologies
with its own significance (general fertility and strength).

Some mention the kinship of the English *boar* and *bear* or the Dutch *bear*
as a sign of natural power. Names with *"Bir"* and *"Ber"* would also refer to
it (as in Brigit who had a cult of her own). The Celtic Cailleach was also
called *Bheur.*

Gungnir

Gungnir (also **Gungni, Gungner**, or **Gungrir**) was the magical spear of chief god Odin in the Northern mythologies of Europe. This spear with a snake in its tip was his weapon of justice. Odin is often depicted with this spear in his hand and on his shoulders the ravens Huginn (Thought) and Muninn (Memory).

Gungnir is a spear that never misses its mark and among the berserkers symbolizes strength.Gungnir is often sung of as "the spear that frightens her enemies and gives Odin's warriors strength.

This spear had been made by the sons of Ivaldi, the dwarves, under Dvalinn the blacksmith's dwarf. It was obtained as a reparation by the joke god Loki from the dwarves along with a wig of gold thread that he had once ordered to replace the golden hair of Thor's wife Sif that he had cut off.

Heimdall

Also spelled Heimdal or Heimdallr.

Guardian god

Heimdall or **Heimdallr** (Hallinskidi, Gullintanni, "with golden teeth") is the guardian of the gods in Nordic mythology. He is the son of nine virgin sisters, daughters of Aegir. Snorri Sturluson names Odin as his father.

Heimdall arises from the foam of the surf. From the mist vapor he creates a connecting arc from Midgard to Asgard, called Bifröst, consisting of vapor and light. Heimdal has absolute hearing, hears the grass and wool grow, and blows the Gjallar horn.

As guardian of the gods, Heimdall needs less sleep than a bird. He is able to see a hundred miles away at night as well as during the day.

Heimdall is called the white god because his skin is whiter than that of any other god. His teeth are golden. Sometimes he takes the form of a ram (often a symbol of strength and fertility in mythology, preferably among nomadic peoples). His horse is called Gulltoppr; his residence, located near the rainbow bridge Bifröst, is Himinbjorg. He possesses a horn, called Gjallar horn or Gjall, whose sound is audible in all nine worlds (cf. Nordic cosmogony), and which at the dawn of Ragnarok will echo loudly throughout everything.

He is not always on guard: according to the myths, this is not strictly necessary because, after all, he can foretell the future; he has therefore for a time deposited his horn with Mímir, at the foot of Yggdrasil. It is also said that he co-drinks in his hall, and that he attends the meetings of the gods.

Possibly there is a special bond between Heimdall and Freya. According to one version of the myth, when her necklace Brinsingamen is stolen by Loki, it is Heimdall who pursues Loki; both gods fight each other in the guise of seals. When the giant Þrymr steals Thor's hammer and demands Freya's hand as a ransom, it is Heimdall who persuades the gods not to give in but, by way of ruse, to send Thor after the giant disguised as a bride.

The way he defends Freya may indicate that Heimdall belongs to the Vanir. The battle with Loki over Brisingamen is not their only confrontation. Both gods are arch rivals; they will be the last to remain at Ragnarok and kill each other.

Father of people and classes

According to the *Rígsþula*, Heimdall has alliance with fertility: he is the father of men and the founder of their classes or castes:

- To Ái (*great-grandfather*) and Edda (*great-grandmother*) he fathered Þræll ("servant"), an ugly child with tanned skin. He had to perform manual labor throughout his life, and the servants descended from him.
- To Afi (*grandfather*) and Amma (*grandmother*), Heimdall fathered Karl ("man," "farmer"), a boy with shining eyes and pink skin. Who grew up to cultivate and build the land.
- And to Faðir (*father*) and Móðir (*mother*) he begot Jarl ("prince"), a boy with shining eyes, light skin and blond hair, to whom he bestowed the runes. From him the nobles descended.

Hell

Goddess of the dead and ruler of the underworld

*The English word hell comes from the name of this
Norse goddess*

Hel (also called **Hella**, **Helle**, **Hell**, **Hela** or **Hellia**) in Nordic mythology is the goddess of the underworld, Helheim and Niflheim.

She is a daughter of Loki and Angrboda and the sister of Fenrisulfr and Jormungand.

Odin cast Hel into the underworld and gave her authority over those who died a natural death. She has a body that is half black and half covered with flesh. Her dwelling place is the Eliudnir Hall, her servants are Ganglati and Ganglot.

In the Edda, Hel is described as the fortune-teller who foretells Baldr's death to Wodan. She also foretells the birth of a son of Wodan, who will avenge Baldr's death. Wodan insults Hel, and she will never let a man come to her again until the downfall of the gods, by the ransomed Loki.

Hermod went on Odin's eight-legged horse Sleipnir to the castle of Hel to free his brother Baldr and his wife Nanna from death.

Hell (location)
The name of the world of the dead

Helheim or **Helgard,** in Nordic mythology, is the underworld where the god Loki's daughter Hel resides. In Snorri Sturluson's Prose-Edda, it is described as a space filled with the shuddering shadow-spooks of those who have died lackluster from illness or old age. Helheim is also the place for dishonorable oath-breakers. It is very cold in this lowest sphere of the universe. It is located at the bottom of Yggdrasil's third root, near Hvergelmir and Náströnd. There is no certainty whether Helheim and Niflheim are very different places, whether one is part of the other, and whether both are different names for the same space or state.

It is said that Helheim is a hall or hall with a roof interwoven with serpentine vertebrae from which poison drips down on those who wade in rivers of blood below. Those who are lost in these halls are given nothing but goat urine to quench their thirst. The gates are said to lie to the south, turned away from Asgard which is said to be located northward.

The hall is surrounded by a river Gjöll, cold as freezing water with people flowing around in it.This river rises in the source Hvergelmir and completely surrounds Helheim. It shows resemblance to the Greco-Roman Styx.

The only way to cross the river is along a golden bridge guarded by a shadow maiden, the giantess Móðguðr, and Garmr (compare Kerberos), a monstrous hellhound who keeps watch with him. They prevent no one from entering, only from returning. If any living person should set foot on the bridge, it rings and reverberates as if a thousand men stepped across it, but the dead touch over it without a tick.

The giant Hræsvelgr (Corpse Eater) sits at the edge of the world above. He sometimes takes the form of an eagle, flapping its wings and bringing forth the ice wind from the realm of the dead.

The dragon Níðhöggr feeds in the depths on the corpses of deceased oathbreakers, first torn apart by wolves.

The underworld (Helheim and Niflheim - *icy hell* or *mist realm*) itself is sometimes called Hell, but this realm of the dead is not comparable to the Christian hell. Not only do murderers or others come there to be punished, and it is not especially a terrible place. Anyone who is not brought to the halls of Freya or Odin, Sessrumnir and Valhalla respectively, by the Walkuren because of outstanding bravery ends up at Hel. That means the sick, the elderly, women and men who had died a natural death.

Garmr (a hellhound) guards the gate of the vestibule Gnipahellir.

The word hell comes from the primeval Germanic word *haljæ*, meaning realm of the dead or underworld.

Hermod

Hermod or **Hermóðr** was a son of Odin and Frigg in Nordic mythology and acted as a messenger of the gods. He went on Odin's eight-legged horse Sleipnir to the castle of Hel to free his brother Baldr from death.

Hlidskjalf

The name **Hlidskjalf** in Nordic mythology refers to Odin's seat or throne. It is located in the realm of Gladsheimr, in the hall Valaskjálf, the great silver-encrusted abode of Odin built by the gods. This abode is located in Asgard, the upper world where the Ashes are at home.

Around *Hlidskjalf, there are* 12 other seats in *Valaskjálf that are* dedicated to the other gods. But *Hlidskjalf* is apparently the most special. It is the seat that gives a view of all worlds. One can also observe all kinds of details from there if one wants to.

In fact, only Odin himself may sit on this throne, but often his wife Frigg sits next to him.

Once Freyr had sat on *Hlidskjalf* and thus surveyed the entire world, until somewhere in the giant land of Jötenheim he spotted a virgin beauty making her way from her father's house to her own room. This aroused such a strong desire in him that Skirnir, Freyr's servant, then had to be persuaded by father Njord to go and talk to Freyr in order to bring him out of his somewhat paralyzing enthusiasm.

Hod

God of winter and darkness

Hodr, in Nordic mythology, was a son of Odin.

The name *Hodr* is Old Norse and means "warrior, fighter." The pronunciation is approximately [hɔðr]? or [hœðr]? . The modern Icelandic form is *Höður*, modernized forms include, for example, *Hod* or *Höd*.

According to the Gylfaginning and the Skaldskaparmál, he was blind. He was the brother of Baldr. By a ruse of Loki, the blind Höðr killed his brother Baldr by shooting him, supposedly invulnerable, with an arrow made from the mistletoe. At that time, the mistletoe was the only creature that could harm Baldr. That was Baldr's Achilles' heel. Baldr, by the way, was avenged by his half-brother Vali, a son of Odin and Rind.

After the Ragnarok, Baldr and Höðr would rise fraternally in a new world.

The Danish writer Saxo Grammaticus (c. 1150 - 1220) calls Hodr *Hötherus* (in the *Gesta Danorum*). The one who plays the role of Vali and avenges Baldr is here called *Bous* and is a son of Óðinn and Rinda.

According to Georges Dumézil, there are similarities with Indian myths. According to him, this is an ancient Indo-European motif.

Hoenir

Also spelled Hænir.

God of silence, spirituality, poetry, and of passion

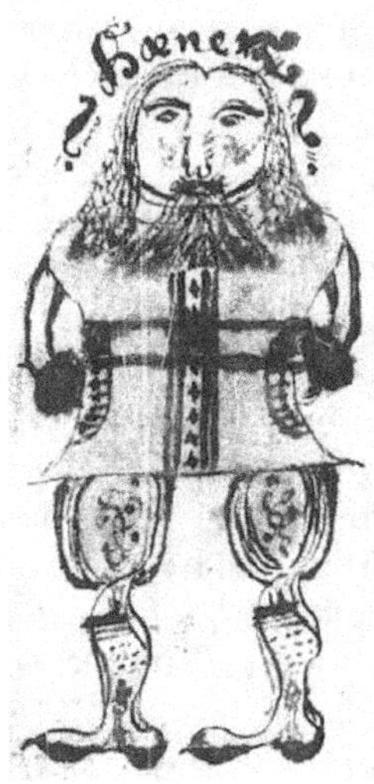

In Germanic mythology, **Hœnir** was an Ase. Like Mímir, he went to the Vanir as a hostage to seal an agreement. The Vanir made Hœnir one of their members, but he suffered from indecision and always relied on Mímir and only gave noncommittal answers when Mímir was absent. This is told in the *Ynglingesaga*

In *Völuspá*, at the creation of the first peoples, Ask and Embla, Hœnir and Lóðurr help the creator god Odin. In *Gylfaginning*, on the other hand, Vili and Vé are mentioned in the place. Since Snorri Sturluson knew the *Völuspá*, it is possible that **Hœnir** was another name for Vili. Always according to the Völuspá, Hœnir was one of the few gods who go on to survive the Ragnarök. Hœnir also has a smaller role in *Haustlöng* and *Reginsmál*.

Hringhorni

A **hringhorni** (Old Norse for: "ship with a circle in the mast") is a ship of
the god Baldr and is described as the *largest of all ships*.

After Baldr is killed by Hodr with an arrow made of mistletoe by Loki, Baldr
is laid to rest on his ship by the other gods. However, when they wanted to
launch him and burn his ship, the gods were unable to launch the ship.
However, with the help of the ancient giantess Hyrrokkin (who came riding
on a wild wolf, with vipers as reins) they succeeded, but she pushed the
ship into the water with such force that the ship ignited and the earth
shook.

Baldr's wife, Nanna, was also burned, having died of grief (or thrown
herself full of grief into the fire). Odin placed his ring Draupnir (a gold ring
that split into nine identical rings once every nine days) in the flames. The
ring was later brought back from hell by Hermod when Hermod later made
his way to hell on Sleipnir (Odin's eight-legged horse) to free Baldr and
Nanna from death, in which, however, he did not succeed.

At the same time as Hringhorni, Litr, a dwarf, was also burned. This dwarf
bucked at Thor's feet as the latter consecrated the flames of the fire with
his hammer Mjolnir. Thor then kicked the dwarf into the fire.

Huginn and Muninn

Huginn and Muninn are the two ravens of Odin in Nordic mythology. Sometimes the last *n* is omitted when writing both names.

Huginn (thoughts) and Muninn (memory) depart daily from Asgard and fly over all nine worlds of Nordic mythology. At the end of the day, they return to Asgard, sit on Odin's shoulders and whisper all the news from the various worlds into his ears.

Huginn and Muninn are also mentioned in the Edda. The Grímnismál narrates:

> *Throughout the world wide, every day,*
> *Flies Huginn and Muninn.*
> *I fear Huginn is not returning home,*
> *For Muninn, I fear even more.*

The name Hugin is etymologically related to the Dutch words *memory* and *heugen*. The name Muninn is etymologically related to the Dutch word "menen" and the English word *mind*.

Hvergelmir

Hvergelmir (rustling or roaring cauldron) was in Nordic mythology a spring in Niflheim. In Nordic and in Celtic mythology, the term *cauldron* often symbolizes a cosmic space, if necessary the universe itself (compare Cailleach).

From *Hvergelmir* flowed eleven poisonous streams, which bore the collective name Elivágar. Separately they were Svöl, Gunurd, Formfimbul, Þul, Slíd, Hríd, Sylg, Ylg, Víd, Leiptr and Gjöll, with Gjöll close to the lowest point, Niflhel. They formed ice in the northern space of Ginnungagap in prehistoric times, when the earth did not exist. The ice was melted by the fire from Muspelheim in the south and life arose there, from which the primal giant Ymir and primal cow Audhumla rose. By sacrificing the primal giant, Odin and his two brothers created the world.

There were other sources that fed the cosmic tree Yggdrasil, Urdarbrunnr (source of Urd) and Mimisbrunnr (source of Mimir), each with its own function in Nordic cosmogony. In the source Hvergelmir there were many snakes as well as the dragon Nidhogg, who gnawed on the extreme root of Yggdrasil there.

Idunn

Also spelled Idun, Ithunn, Ithun, or Iduna.

Goddess of spring and rejuvenation

In Nordic mythology, **Iðunn** is the keeper of the apples of youth, which gave the gods eternal youth.

The name *Iðunn* is Old Norse and means "the rejuvenated one." The pronunciation is approximately [ˈiðunː][?] . Modernized forms of the name are *Iduna* and *Idun*.

Iðunn, according to the Gylfaginning, is Bragi's wife.

Iðunn was once kidnapped by the giant Þjazi (Thjazi). Loki helped him finish the job. In fact, Loki was disguised as a falcon and was thus captured by the giant. The giant knew it was no ordinary falcon, imprisoned him and starved him. He forced him to say his name and help him kidnap Iduna. Loki finally agreed.

The gods did not immediately notice that Iðunn was gone until they noticed that they were aging. Eventually they found out the score, as Loki had aged considerably less. In fact, Loki had taken an apple from Iðunn, so he stayed younger a little longer. Loki confessed everything and then helped the gods get Iðunn and her apples back by tricking the giant into turning Iðunn into a nut (or swallow) and then reappearing in Asgard.

Iðunn is mentioned before Christianization only in Þjóðólfr of Hvinir's (Thjódolf) skalden poem *Haustlöng* (around 900). Snorri Sturluson uses this poem in the Gylfaginning. In addition, Iðunn occurs in the LokÆsirna. Otherwise, there are no surviving texts that say anything about Iðunn. If she was a goddess, then not a very famous one, but as the story outlined above indicates, an important one for the Æsir.

Jörmungandr

The **Midgaard snake** or **Jǫrmungandr** (sometimes also *Jormungand* or *Jorgmungander*), as a snake, is virtually the largest and most dangerous monster in Nordic mythology. He is one of the three children of Loki and Angrboða and probably the most terrifying.

The Midgaardsnake is so huge that it lies in a circle around Midgard, the world. Its head reaches to the tip of its tail and when it bites into it (Like the Ouroboros) it shakes with rage, causing earthquakes.

His archenemy is Thor, with whom he will engage in a life and death struggle during the Ragnarok (the end of times that is the final battle). Thor almost captured him once before, but because his companion became afraid, he failed to kill the unbeast.

Thor, together with the giant Hymir, sailed so far up the primeval sea that even the giant became frightened. Using an ox head as bait, he tried to catch the snake. When it bit, it gave such a hard yank that Thor's fists landed on the daggerboard with a crash. With his axial strength he braced himself so that both feet went through the boat and landed with it on the seabed. Thus he pulled the snake to the edge in the meantime. And the fiercer Thor looked at the snake in the depths, the fiercer she hurled venom back at him. Hymir drew white as the snake undulated over his boat. He cut the cord with his fishing knife just as Thor swung his hammer in the air. The snake sank back into the sea, but Thor threw the hammer after it, and it struck the snake's head off at the bottom, but that is only according to men (according to the Edda), for the snake is said to be alive in the ocean of the world. Thor had only struck Hymir's ear with his hammer, so that the latter went overboard - his soles can still be seen in the sea.

Jǫrmungandr will be crushed by the lightning god and his Mjölnir, but he himself will perish from his poison.

Jǫrmungandr still has Fenrir as a brother and Hel as a sister, also descendants of Loki and the giantess Angrboða.

Jötun

A supernatural being

Jötun (Old Norse: Jötnar, Jöten or Jøtnar, Jøten) or **Thursen** (þursar) are, in Nordic mythology, giants with awesome power and of enormous dimensions. They are humanoid or beast-like entities of often unimaginable dimensions (greater than those of the gods), and gifted with almost divine strength and power.

The giants often quarrel with the gods. In the process, they are either very stupid (especially in the *Heroic Sagas*, possibly as a contrast to the new heroes) or, on the contrary, very wise because of their advanced age (especially in the original pre-Christian pagan times). The giants span all time-space with their unique knowledge. Since they are from prehistoric times, they are also attributed great original wisdom and unique knowledge.

They are represented in many different guises, sometimes with multiple heads, (three, six or nine).

Name meaning

Jötun probably has the same origin as *food*, compare also the Old English *eóten*, and had the original meaning "glutton" or "man-eater."

Risar (sing. *risi*), especially *bergrisar*, is probably related to *rijzen*, and means a "rijzig figure," a "giant."

Thursar or þursar (sing. þurs), especially *hrímþursar* (Vorstreuzen) may be derived from "thirst" or "bloodlust," cf. Old High German *duris* or *thuris*. Old English also has the related word þyrs with the same meaning. A bloodthirsty ancient Finnish war god was called *Tursas*; the Finnish language was one of the oldest in the Nordic region.

"Thurs" is also the name of the rune Þ, which later evolved into the letter Þ.

A giantess could also be referred to as a *gýgr*.

Origin of giants

They are all descendants of the hermaphroditic primordial giant Ymir and they arose before the gods, who are in fact also their descendants. *Ymir* is the name of the first life that formed in the beginning of time. It was the terrifying rijpreus, created from rijp deposits in the original chaotic void (known as Ginnungagap). During his sleep, the primordial giant became something like a growing plant and from his armpits emerged a giant son and a giant daughter, and by copulation of his two feet, a six-headed monster Thrudgelmir was created. These three entities together produced the race of *hrímþursar*, who populated the original realm of Niflheim, world of frost and mist.

The gods (Ashes and Vans), on the other hand, claim to have evolved from a certain Búri, another giant.

Then, when Ymir is sacrificed by Odin, Vili and Ve (three grandchildren of Búri) as material for the construction of the other worlds, Niflheim is completely engulfed by its lifeblood (*blood* or water), and in the process all the giants perish except two, a certain giant Bergelmir and his spouse, from which their kind is reborn.

Remarkably, most of the gods are directly descended from giants and giantesses, or conversely, certain giants are accepted as gods. Giants and gods often quarrel with each other, although some help each other. Loki, the fire god, for example, is half Jote and also has a dual nature.

Residence

An important residence of the Jötuns is Utgard Castle in Jötunheim, beyond Midgard, the human world, from which it is separated by high mountains with dense forests. Jotunheim is one of the nine worlds in Nordic cosmogony. The overlord of Utgard is Utgardloki, whose realm coincides with the realm of the dead. When giants live in worlds other than their own they prefer to keep themselves in caves and dark places.

The Fire Giants, on the other hand, live in the fire kingdom of Muspelheim, one of the nine worlds in the Nordic cosmogony. The fire giants are descendants of Muspel and Surt. The human world was protected from the giants by the rampart the gods had made from Ymir's eyebrows. The other worlds were separated from those of the fire giants by the bridge Bifrost, which the giants could not enter without collapsing.

Character of giants

Unlike the Ashes who represent order, the Jötuns are the forces of chaos in Norse mythology. They are untamed and represent the forces of original chaos and of untamed destructive nature.

Most of the giants represent aspects of natural violence, such as:

- Vorstreuzen/driving giants
- Water and Ocean Giants
- Fire Giants
- Air and Storm Giants
- Mountain and Stone Giants
- Forest Giants

Giants are often terrifying because of their inhuman appearance. Giants are described with claws, tusks, black skin and distinctive sizes of limbs. There are those with multiple heads as well as non-human forms. For example, Jǫrmungandr and Fenrir were descendants of Loki and Angrboða, a giantess, and these did not resemble human beings in any way. Hel, on the other hand, did again, were it not for the fact that half of her body was half decomposed.

With the terrifying appearance go such traits as naiveté and weak intellect. The Edda often compares the intellect of giants to that of children; emotional and not rational. Yet individually named or more narrowly defined giants are often given opposite characteristics. Being unbelievably old, they carry the wisdom of times gone by, such as Vafthrúðnir and Mímir. And it is these that Odin seeks out to gain pre-cosmic knowledge.

Relationship with the gods

Most of the giants are considered dangerous or even evil and enemies of gods (Axes and Vans) and humans, but there are also good-natured giants.

Many spouses of gods are giants. Njǫrð is married to Skaði, Gerðr becomes the wife of Frey, Odin wins the love of Gunnlod, and even Thor, the great slaughterer of the species, loves Jarnsaxa (giantess), the mother of Magni. In this way, they come across as sort of lesser deities, something that can also be said of the giant Ægir, who has far more connections to the gods than to the scum that populate Jotunheim. None of these fear the light, and their dwelling places do not differ much from those of the gods in terms of comfort.

But the relationship between giants and gods or humans is favorable only with some (as with Ägir and Mímir), and other Jötuns pose a threat to the Axis. Consequently, they are constantly engaged in a cosmic war, in which Thor (calling with his hammer to order) takes the upper hand, and this lasts until the Ragnarök.

Ragnarök

Until the Ragnarök, Heimdall permanently guards the Bifröst Bridge between Ásgard and Jötunheim. Thor often goes to Jötunheim to kill as many of the giants as possible with his hammer.

The evil giants of these genera (most of them) will go to war against the Ashes at the end of time. The fire giant Surt (possibly the only being even older than Ymir) will then destroy all of creation with his flaming sword.

Their defeat by the three god-brothers Odin, Vili and Vé represents the victory of culture over nature, although it results in its downfall.

Giants in later Scandinavian folklore

In later times, giants became known as trolls in Scandinavia. They cannot tolerate the sound of church bells and must therefore live far from civilization, in the mountains or in the farthest forests. If they do sometimes come to the human community, it is mainly to silence church bells by throwing large rolling boulders on church buildings.

The giants were considered a race of the past, whose remains could still be seen in the landscape. Saxo Grammaticus attributed the raising of dolmens to the giants. A large boulder seemingly lost in the landscape was called a "giant throw." This term survived in a story from Swedish folklore, as if a giant in older times had torn away two pieces of land creating Lake Väner and Lake Vätter, and thrown them into the Baltic Sea, where they now form the islands of Gotland and Öland, respectively.

Jötunheimr

Jotunheim or **Jötunheim** (Old Norse **Jötunheimr** or, plural,
Jötunheimar) is the homeland of the Jötun in Nordic mythology.
Jotunheim is described in the Prose-Edda.

There is also a mountain area located in southern Norway, where it is
called **Jotunheimen**.

The origins of Jotunheim

First the giants inhabited the Vigrid Plain, where Ymir and the first gods
were also born. Odin and his brothers Vili and Vé sacrificed Ymir to make
the worlds.

All but two Hrimthursar drowned in Ymir's life fluid. Bergelmir (son of
Thrudgelmir, grandson of Ymir) and his wife were able to crawl into a
hollow tree stump in time to use it as a boat. Bergelmir then sailed with his
wife to a place that would come to be called Jotunheim. There they rose
and brought forth a new younger lineage of Hrimthursar. Thus Bergelmir
became the primordial father of a new generation of giants, the Jötun. This
progeny harbored a deep hatred for the Axis.

Bergelmir's fortunes put him on a par with countless Flood heroes who
escaped general drowning. There are the Mesopotamian Utnapisthim,
Deukalion and Pyrrha, Philemon and Baucis in the Greek myths, the Bible
has Noah who survived the flood in an ark.

Separation from Yggdrasil

To prevent Thursen and Jötun from overrunning the world of men and
gods, the gods built a rampart around Midgard and Asgard that was made
of Ymir's eyebrows. Thus they separated the world tree Yggdrasil from
Jotunheim (with the giant fortress Útgard at the far end).

Until the Ragnarok, when their rage truly erupts, the Jötun will be hostile to
the gods this act in mind, though there will be magnanimous giants. But
then they will storm Asgard from Niflhel.

Residents and visitors

In Jotunheim lived (among others);

- Þrymr (who had stolen Thor's hammer Mjöllnir) in his abode Thrymheim,
- Thjazi (whose daughter Skadi became an Asin) also lives in Thrymheim,
- Menglad in his castle Gastropnir.

Thor liked to travel to Jotunheim, as there he could practice his favorite sport: beating giants to death with his hammer Mjöllnir.

Loki once stayed with the giantess Angrboða, with whom he had three children (Jörmungandr, Hel and Fenrir - they play a major role during the Ragnarok). He went to Jotunheim more often, until he was tied up by the Ashes under Jörmungandr's dripping mouth.

Thor and Loki in Jotunheim

There is a story in the Prose Edda that deals with a period when ice formation occurred; which ice age is meant is unclear. The story has similarities with *Hymisvädet*, in which a cooking pot is sought. Loki in both stories is the instigator of a forbidden act, after which Thor's revenge comes upon the perpetrator.

As in *Vafþrúðnismál* (*Song of Vafthrudnir*), a visit by Thor and Loki illustrates the illusion that constitutes consciousness in the world of giants.

The story

The ice age destroyed the harvest and killed man and beast. Thor went with Loki to Räsvälg to complain. Thor's chariot cannot cross Bifröst, so they wade through the river Ifing (doubt). In Midgard they stay with a poor farmer and his children Tjalfe (speed) and Röskva (work). There is little food so Thor slaughters his goats Tandgniostr and Tandgrisnir (teeth grinder and teeth grinder) and tells the others to put the bones in their skins unbroken.

Loki whispers to a farmer's son that he must taste the marrow, and so the son breaks a bone. In the morning, Thor revives his goats with a blow of his hammer, but discovers that one goat is paralyzed. The farmer offers that his children will become Thor's servants, and Tjalfe accompanies Thor and Loki on their journey.

They spend the night in a strange structure with a small and a large room, and they hear a rumbling sound. The next morning they find a sleeping giant, Skrimir. The house was his glove and the roar his snoring. The gods try to open the giant's bag, but are unsuccessful. Thor then strikes the giant three times with his hammer, but the giant does not awaken. There are still three valleys cleaving the mountain where the giant slept.

The party reaches Utgárdloki (Loki of the outer court) and are challenged to a series of races. Tjalfe enters a race, but loses. Loki claims to eat more than any giant, but loses because the giant also eats the plate. Thor wants to empty a drinking horn, but can only lower the level in the giant's barrel a little. Then Thor has to lift the giant's cat, but only manages to move one paw. Thor then wants to wrestle with the giants, but the giants' elderly nanny defeats him with ease.

The gods leave for their own sphere and the host accompanies them and explains the illusions. Tjalfe has the speed of lightning, but could not beat thinking. Loki took on Logi (flame) who also ate the wooden board. The horn had its end in the depths of the ocean and the world of giants had shaken with fear as the level of the water dropped. The cat was Jörmungandr (equator) and this one had moved alarmingly. Elli, the elderly nanny, is in reality old age and exhausts everyone.

Thor raises his hammer in anger and wants to avenge himself with a trick, but he stands on a plain that stretches endlessly and his host and the city are gone.

Loki

God of fire, magic, shapeshifting, and chaos

Loki (also *Looki*, *Loke*, *Lopt* or *Loptr*) is the god of chaos and lies from Nordic mythology.

He is a troublemaker and a shapeshifter. He helps other gods, but also often works against them. After he had a hand in the death of the god Balder, the other gods decided to imprison him. He was tied up in a cave with the entrails of his own son, and a snake was hung over his head whose venom dripped onto his face. Here he would remain until Ragnarok, the end of the world. In the ensuing war, he would fight the other gods and Heimdall and himself would meet each other's end.

Genealogy

Loki was one of the sons of Farbauti and Laufey and blood brother of Odin.

Loki married twice, first to the giantess Angrboda who gave him three
monstrous creatures: Fenrir, the Midgaard snake (or: Jǫrmungandr) and
Hel (queen of the underworld). Actually, Loki's daughter's name is Leikinn
or Leikn and she is the goddess of disease, and Niflhel (or: "Not Hel") is
none other than the foul goddess Urd. He then married Sigyn, who gave
him two sons: Vali and Narvi. These sons played a role in his capture. In
fact, these sons never existed, for Narvi (Nidhadr, Mimir) is none other
than Mimir, and Vali is the son of Odin and Rindr. It was Mimir's chains
that were used to bind Loki, referring to Vali's chains that kept him from
killing Hodr, or the womb of his own mother Rindr.

Loki is also the mother of Sleipnir, as he had then taken the form of a
(gray) mare and was then impregnated by the stallion Svadilfari, the horse
of the vorstreus.

His exploits

Loki, in creating the worlds, gives colors to the bridge Bifröst, which
Heimdall made, and makes it into a rainbow. The world is then ready and
man can appear there (verses 17-18 of the Voluspá).

His evil disposition may have stemmed from the fact that his parents were
frost giants. He could not resist playing daring pranks and endangering the
gods, although he often saved them again thanks to his cunning. For
example, he once brought about the kidnapping of Iduna, causing the
gods to age rapidly. Sometimes he endangered his comrade Thor, even
though he also helped him recover his hammer as recounted in the
Þrýmskviða.

When constructing Asgaard, he fooled the frost giant Hrimthur who had to
build a wall around it, and only received his pay from the Æsir if he
finished the job on time. Loki turned himself into a mare and thus lured
away Svadilfari,the vorstreus' horse, with the result that the vorstreus
himself ran after it to get his horse back. From being with that stallion
came Sleipnir, the eight-legged horse destined for Odin.

In the Reginsmál, "the song of Regin," Regin tells Siegfried about Odin,
Hoenir and Loki. They had come to the waterfall from the dwarf Vigilant,
who lived there as a pike. Otter, the brother of Regin and Fafnir, was
devouring a salmon there, when Loki threw him to death with a stone.
They stripped his skin off. At the court of Hreidmar, the father of Regin,
Fafnir and Otter, the gods were captured. They had to cover the otter's
skin with gold inside and out. Loki had to go for the gold. Loki caught the

pike Vigilant and took all his gold from him. With that, the otter skin was covered and the gods were set free. Fafnir killed his father and appropriated all the gold, after which Regin induced Siegfried to kill the dragon Fafnir and appropriate his treasures.

After the death of Balder and Hödur, the sea giant Aegir sets up a feast in his cave. At that feast, as described in the LokÆsirna, Loki goes too far in his insult to the other gods, so they decide to imprison him. Loki knows the time has come, and sits on a barren mountain to watch them arrive. When the gods come, he turns himself into a salmon. The gods make a net to catch him, but he dodges it first. At sea, however, sea monsters and fish led by Njord and Aegir await him. Loki flees back over the net, but Thor is faster and grabs him.

To put an end to his wickedness, he is tied up under the dripping mouth of a venomous snake (one of his children). Loki was terribly bored there. He was waiting for Ragnarok, in which he would lead the forces of evil against the gods. He himself finally died at the hands of Heimdall.

Character and meaning

Loki is an ambiguous and mysterious figure:According to the Gylfaginning, he is an Ase and he often fights with them against the giants. Through dwarves he has magical objects forged such as the hammer Mjölnir for Thor and the ring Draupnir for Odin. But at the same time he is proud of his murder of Balder and is the father of infernal beings.

Often he is also recognized as a hero of culture, akin to the Greek Prometheus. The fire that this one bestows on men is an ambiguous gift: on the one hand, culture-promoting (heat, light, cooking, metalwork...), on the other, culture-killing when it turns out that man cannot in fact control it (firearms, technology).

However, although according to some mainstream theories, he is seen as a fire spirit, with all the potential for good and evil that goes along with fire, it could be that this view can be traced back to a linguistic contamination with *logi* "fire," for there is very little indication of this in the myth, where Loki's role is primarily associated with Odin, either as his willing equal or as his antagonist.

Ström even identifies the two gods to the extent of calling Loki a "hypostasis of Odin. And Rübekeil suggests that the two gods were originally identical, derived from the Celtic Lugus or Lugh (whose name would be contained in *Loki*). In any case, the figure of Loki was probably not a late invention of the Nordic skalds, but rather descended from a common Indo-European prototype.

Dr. Jan de Vries saw in Loki a mythical figure akin to the North American trickster, an ambivalent being, even in his attitude toward humans.

For Georges Dumézil, Loki is an archetypal figure of ever-present deceit and malice, and his presence among the enemies of the gods during the eschatological battle make him a homologue of Duryodhana from the Indian Mahabharata epic. There Duryodhana is the personification of the zeitgeist of the age of decay and downfall (Kali Yuga), which in Nordic mythology corresponds to the concept of Fimbulvetr.

That the number 13 passes as an unlucky number may have been derived from a saga surrounding Loki in which he appears as the 13th, uninvited guest at a feast and then plunges the world into mourning.

Loki had no temples nor cult.

Midgard

Midgard (middle realm) is the name of the human realm in Nordic mythology. This world is located somewhere in the middle of Yggdrasil and is surrounded by a world of water or a primordial ocean, which cannot be crossed. In this primordial ocean lives the world snake, which is so gigantic that it encircles the entire world and bites its own tail.

In Nordic mythology, *Miðgarðr* was applied to an area walled by a rampart built from the eyebrows of the primordial being Ymir, which was to protect the world from the violence of the Jötun living in Jötenheim.

Localization

Midgard is an intermediate world, located below the heavenly Asgaard and above the hellish world of Niflheim. Together, these three form the triad of upper world, middle world and underworld.

Asgard is right above the position held by Midgard in Yggdrasil, and is the world of gods, more specifically that of the Ashes. Other deities, the Wans, resided in Wanaheim.

Origin of Midgard

Midgard was created from the body of the Vorstreus Ymir (which means "twin" or "hermaphrodite" in Old Norse); he was, according to Norse mythology, the first living creature created from the drops of water that emerged from the melting ice that filled the Ginnungagap (gaping void). From his body, Odin and his brothers made Midgard. From the giant's flesh they made the land and from his lifeblood the seas. Midgard was connected to Asgard by the Bifrost Bridge, which was guarded by Heimdall.

End of Midgard

According to legend, Midgard will be destroyed in the Ragnarok, in the battle that will take place at the end of time. Then the World Serpent will rise from the primordial ocean and penetrate land and sea with its venom, so that the sea will boil and engulf the land. After the final battle that will take place on the Vigrid Plain, Midgard and all its life forms will be destroyed as the earth sinks into the sea.

Muspelheim

Muspelheim ("Flame Country"), also **Muspel** (*Old Norse Múspellsheimr and Múspell, respectively*) is the world of fire in Nordic mythology. It is the homeland of the Fire Giants and their master Surt.

The heat of this world contrasts sharply with the icy cold of the opposite Niflheim, and where at the beginning of time these two worlds meet in the yawning chasm, the Ginnungagap, violent processes occur, melting the ice of Nifleim into water, and causing sparks from Muspelheim to fly away, giving birth to stars, comets and planets.

Both worlds, according to the Old Norse creation story, arose from the will of Fimbultyr in the endless world ground (Ginnungagap), where they finally contribute to the creation of Ymir, thus making the existence of matter possible.

Muspelheim, according to some, is named after Muspell ("the World Walker") and is inhabited by Muspell's sons, of whom Surt ("Black") is the captain. According to others, Surt would be just another name for Muspel.

In any case, under Surt's leadership, the giants would unleash the final battle in the Ragnarok against the gods. Surt and his sons would then first enter the bridge Bifröst, but it would succumb to their trampling. Finally, Surt would dissolve the worlds into fire with his flaming sword Surtalogi, beginning with Yggdrasil, the Measure Tree, World Tree or Sacred Ash.

Muspelheim is so long separated from Midgaard by Myrkviðr ("gloomy forest"), a dark, impenetrable forest that also symbolizes the psychological boundary between good and evil.

Naglfar

Naglfar is a ship from Nordic mythology made from the nails of the dead.

One cut the nails of the just deceased, to prevent this death ship, located at Nástrond, from coming off faster than was necessary. This was because Naglfar would sail to Midgard with the Ragnarok, causing the downfall of the gods. The ship will be piloted by Hrym, according to Snorri Sturluson in the Gylfaginning, or by Loki, as stated in the Völuspá.

It is also said in the Völuspá that this boat is sailed by "munu Muspells," Muspels people. Although muspilli in Old High German and Old Saxon means something along the lines of the end of the world, the Norse poet took it to mean the name of a giant.

Nanna

Goddess associated with joy, peace, and the moon

Nanna in Nordic mythology is the wife of Baldr, mother of Forseti and daughter of Nepr. She is a giantess but becomes Asin after she marries Baldr. When Baldr is killed by his blind brother Höðr, she succumbs to her grief and throws herself on the pyre of his corpse burning on his drifting ship Hringhorn.

Niflheim

Niflheim (dark world) in Nordic mythology is the realm of mists.

In Niflheim, according to some sources, Hell reigned. Niflheim was the realm of the dead, an icy world where a living person had little business. Yet even the gods came here from time to time, for example Balder's brother Hermod made a request to Hel to free Balder from death.

The deepest point of Niflheim is Niflhel, where Hel's castle of the same name stands. Also in Niflheim is the spring of Mímir, which bestows wisdom and for which Odin sacrificed his eye to be allowed to drink from it.

According to the Gylfaginning in Snorri Sturluson's Prose-Edda, in the center of Niflheim is the source Hvergelmir (roaring cauldron), from which eleven poisonous rivers (Elivagar, storm waves) spring. These became, at a great distance from their source, layers of ice in the northern part of the Space, Ginnungagap. Where the ice came into contact with the heat of southern Muspelheim (Flame Land) it melted and life emerged. The forms of the primal giant Ymir and the primal cow Audhumla appeared in it and by sacrificing him Odin and his two brothers created the world.

Njord

Also spelled Njorth, Niord, or Njordr.

God of the sea, the wind, fertility, and patron saint of fishermen and sailors

In Nordic mythology, **Njord** or **Njordr** (Old Norse *Njörðr*) is a god belonging to the Wanen. He represents fertile coastal land, seamanship and the art of sailing.

Name

Njörðr's name is written Njǫrðr in Old Norse but the 'ǫ' is often replaced by 'ö'. So one can convert the name in several ways: *Njord, Njordr, Niord, Niordr, Njörd* and *Njördr*.

Alternative spellings for Njord also include Njördh, Njörðr and Njörður (Icelandic spelling).

Njord is possibly similar to the Roman God of the sea Neptune and the Greek Poseidon.

Genealogy

Njord is the husband of the giantess Skaði and father of Yngvi-Freyr and Freyja. According to the Heimskringla, their mother was Njord's own sister. His sister's name could also be Njord, according to a name reconstruction of a Suevian goddess, which Tacitus transliterated into Latin as "Nerthus"

(= *Njörðr*). He resided in Nóatún ("City of Ships"). Njord is a god closely associated with fertility, as are the other Wans in general.

Njord and his children later came to live with the Æsir, as "hostages" after the war between the two families of gods. Although they were considered part of the family of aristocrats and legitimate leaders, they were not free to leave, so the mutual interests of the peace treaty could be safeguarded.

Njord is the Old Norse equivalent of the goddess Nerthus, described by Tacitus. Thus Hilda R. Ellis Davidson suggested in "Gods and Myths of Northern Europe" (1964) that there may once have been a pairing of gods, Njord and Nerthus, with Freya later replacing Nerthus. She also states that there were more male and female gods paired in Norse mythology, but of which we know little more than their names (e.g., Ullr and Ullin).

Comparative mythologist Georges Dumézil elaborated on Jacob Grimm's idea that the hero Hadingus in *Danish History*, Book I of Saxo Grammaticus could be an euphemized (*"historicized"*) version of Njord. This suggestion was used by SF fantasy writer Poul Anderson in his *War of the Gods*.

In Viktor Rydberg's idiosyncratic reconstruction of Nordic mythology, Njord is also known as Fridleif, *the Peaceful One*. With Hodr, he undertook a peace mission to Weland and Egil, who rejected this peace. He later rescued his son Freyr from the hands of the Jötun. During the war of the gods between Æsir and Wanen, he led the attack on Asgard, which he won. During his absence from Vanaheim, Loki tried to take over there, but Njord defeated him in battle and showed him the way out.

Njord and Skaði

According to Rydberg, after stealing the youth's apples, the Æsir accidentally killed Skaði's father, Weland-Thjazi and regretted it. But then, he had brought the Ice Age into the world. Giant daughter Skaði thereupon strapped on her skis, put on her chain mail, put on her helmet and set out for Valhalla to avenge her father. But the gods agreed that they had to make up for the loss somehow. So she was allowed to choose any male god as her husband, but she was only allowed to see their feet when making her choice. She took a long look at all the feet, then chose the cleanest white pair, thinking they would belong to Baldr. But it was not Baldr, it was Njord, for his feet were always washed clean by the sea.And although they loved each other very much, their marriage was somewhat difficult in the end. For Skaði as the daughter of a mountain giant lived in the winter land, and Njord minded always being awakened by the wolves, and it was so already much too cold for him to sleep. And Skaði couldn't stand living in a spring forest and being awakened by singing birds every morning. And she also found it just a little too warm there. So they had decided to take turns living nine nights in one place and nine in the other, in Þrymheimr with her, and then in Nóatún. And so they were still doing fairly well.

Norns

Their names were Urd (also spelled Urdr, or Weird, meaning "Past"), Verdande ("Present"), and Skuld ("Future").

Three female beings who rule the destiny of gods and men

Norns are the arranging or destiny goddesses of Norse mythology who are represented as three sisters who determine the fate of men and gods. As female guardian spirits ("disir"), they lay down the fate of each human and deity at birth. They do this by sketching runes in the tribe of Yggdrasil and according to the belief in certain areas also by weaving. This method is found in the arrangement goddesses of almost all other mythologies such as the Moerae or Moira of Greek mythology. The Norse are quite often confused with the Walkuren, who, however, have a very different role within Norse mythology.

The three Norns are named Urd (what once was), Verdandi (what is born to be) and Skuld (what will be). They live next to the *"well of Urd"* which stood under the tree of life Yggdrasil in Asgard. Urd was the first Norn and represented fate or the past tense. Verdandi (*becoming*) in some sources is said to symbolize the present, Skuld the future. The trio would also maintain the tree of life Yggdrasil by smearing white clay on the ever-rotting wood.

Their characters bear many similarities to similar arrangement goddesses among Romans (Parcae) and Greeks (Moirae) in classical antiquity. Their service partly coincides with that of the presumably from very ancient times and widespread worship of the triple mother goddesses, who can be assumed to have three main functions: as protectors of domestic happiness, as patrons of a settlement or tribe and as arranging goddesses. The major difference from these arrangement goddesses of classical antiquity is that the fate the Norns weave is not final but much more dynamic and leaves much room for the individual to potentially change his fate.

In popular belief, the Norns survived for some time after the introduction of Christianity. In Scandinavian folklore, the "nornae" are still known to the population. Contemporary spiritual groups, New Age and Ásatrú keep that cult alive, often mixed with contemporary beliefs.

Náströnd

In Nordic mythology, **Nástrond** (*Corpse Beach*) is a place in the underworld, the Niflheim, where the death ship Naglfar lies. Nidhogg lives there with his kind and from this shore Naglfar departs with his dead to Midgard during the Ragnarok. Also on Nástrond is the hall of the death goddess Hel, where the evil-doers bear the brunt.

Odin

Also called Othin, Wotan, Woden, Wuotan, Voden, or Votan.

God of wisdom, war, magic, poetry, prophecy, victory, and death

Odin (Old Norse: Óðinn, Swedish and Danish: **Oden**) is considered the supreme god or alfather in Nordic mythology. These forms are derived from Proto-Germanic ***Wōdanaz**, from which also Old Saxon **Wōdan**, Anglo-Saxon **Wōden**.

Odin is the god of knowledge, wisdom, battle, war, the afterlife, magic, medicine and runic writing.

The description of Odin stems primarily from the *Gylfaginning*, a 13th-century narrative by the Icelander Snorri Sturluson, in which the Christian perspective predominates. Older sources such as the *Poetic Edda* present a less unambiguous picture.

According to Snorri, he lives in Gladsheimr but also regularly resides in Valaskjálf (Asgard) where his seat Hlidskjalf offers wide views of the worlds. He has another special hall Walhalla there, with many gates and covered with shields, where he receives all honorably fallen and chosen warriors.

Besides Frigg, his wife, Odin also fathered children by other women. His sons included Donar, Baldr, the blind Hodr (also called Hod or Hodur) and Sigi, the ancestor of the Völsung family, to which also Sigmund and his son Siegfried belonged. In the Prologue of the Prose-Edda, Veggdegg, Saeming and Yngvi (Freyr) are still mentioned as his sons. With Fjorgyn (Earth) he has a son Thor and with a giantess a son Vidar (God of vengeance), who will avenge him in the final battle. With Rindr (winter frozen earth) he has the son Vali.

Recent studies, notably by English linguist Richard North, suggest that the cult of Odin / Wodan did not emerge until well after the Folk Movements. The god Odin would then have adopted the characteristics of earlier gods, especially the fertility god Ynvgi, but also the Christian God. Later Christian authors would retroactively portray him as a negative or pagan mirror image of the Christian god. In particular, Odin's hanging from the tree of life mirrors both the death of Christ on the cross and the death of the traitor Judas, who, like Odin, was depicted hanging from a tree.

The name Odin

The name *Wodan* for an early medieval chief god was common in northwestern Europe: he was rendered as Odin in northern Europe. Wodan is usually equated with the god Mercury, as described by Tacitus in his depiction of the native gods. Presumably, however, the deity Wodan was unknown in Roman times.

The name is derived from Protogermanic *wōdaz*, meaning "rage," "anger" or "ecstasy. The name Odin is closely related to that of another Norse god, Óðr. The Old Norse word óðr indicates 'anger' or 'rage,' but also 'ecstasy,' 'poetry' or even 'universal wisdom,' akin to Old English *wōð* 'song, poem' . *Underlying* this is presumably an Indoeuropean word *wāt^h* - *referring* to 'emotional excitement', 'ecstasy' and 'poetic inspiration'. Derived from this are words such as Latin *uātēs* 'prophet, poet', Old English *fáith* (idem) and *fáth* 'prediction', Welsh *gwawd* 'poem', as well as 'resentment'. Odin is thus associated both with wisdom (knowledge, wisdom, prophecy, poetry and literature) and strength (energy, battle and war).

Supreme knowledge and wisdom

Odin was the most gifted among them, and from him they learned all -at least most- of the arts, for he was the first to master them all. And if one has to explain why Odin was honored so much, it was for the following reasons: when he sat with his friends, he was so beautiful and impressive to behold, that it warmed every one's heart (*Proza-Edda, Gylfaginning*, 7).

Odin in the Edda is the living symbol of supreme power and wisdom. He himself came into being in this capacity through the giant Ymir who was given aspects of a living plant from which grow all kinds of beings such as the giants Búri or Borr and Bestla who themselves produce Odin, Vili and Vé.

> The last three together create Midgard, a world where people can live.
>
> As material for this they use the primal giant Ymir, which is sacrificed by them. (The giant's skull becomes the firmament, carried by four dwarfs: north, south, east and west. The brains become clouds, the bones mountains, etc. Alves turn the giant's blood into water and sea, and his flesh into earth and clay).

Odin has many faces and as many names (fifty in Grimnismal alone). He is also called **Alfather**, because he is one of the creators of the world. He is also called "the wanderer", because he is always on the move and among the people, in order to acquire new knowledge. He can change shape, and thus has many adventures. He does not always have easy characteristics, because besides being wise he is also cunning.

He ceded an eye to the giant Mímir to be allowed to drink from the well of wisdom, and it now lies at the very bottom of the well:

That spring was in the territory of Mímir, who drank from it every day and always played chess against himself. Odin was allowed to drink from the spring on the condition that he would pay a price for it. Odin said that he was willing to give up an eye for it upon which Mímir told him that this, then, was the price he was asking. However, Mímir was not malicious, he just wanted to show that wisdom has its price. He therefore took care of Odin as best he could. Later, when the chief god returned to Asgard, he was accompanied by Mímir, who would henceforth be the councilor of the gods and regularly played a game of chess with Odin. From this adventure Odin kept the name "the One-Eyed One."

His knowledge of the future bedeviled Odin. He also sat with the question he alone knew the answer to, the Odin question. And the Germanic mythological cycle had begun with a bloodbath when Odin and his brothers, Vili and Vé, created the human world from the corpse of the frost giant Ymir, and would end with the bloodbath Ragnarok, where the blood of the giants themselves would flow. The prologue to Ragnarok was the death of Odin's son Baldr, which made the gods realize that Loki's cunning had become a darkened power. Odin cannot prevent the catastrophe. His only solace lies in the knowledge that Baldr will be revered as supreme god in a new land that will rise out of the Urocean.

Baldr comes across as a kind of glorified reissue of Odin: without his little edges.In the *Völsunga saga,* it is told that Odin planted his sword in the amber cane, the oak tree in King Völsung's court. The sword was for whoever could pull it out. Only Sigmund was capable of doing so. When Sigmund fights over damsel Hjördis (Siegfried's mother) with Lyngvi, a son of King Dogson, Odin smashes Sigmund's sword to pieces with a halberd, causing Sigmund to lose. The pieces of Odin's sword are later forged together for Siegfried by the dwarf Regin, and with this sword, Gram, Sigmund's son Siegfried is able to defeat the dragon Fafnir.

Odin's sacrifice

Thus Odin/Wodan tells how he acquired the runes of wisdom:

Nine nights I hung from the tree, wounded by the spear dedicated to Odin. Sacrificed myself to myself.

Hanging from that tree, no one knows where the roots are.

No one gave me bread, no one gave me water. Into the abyss I peered to grasp the runes, with a loud cry and I lost consciousness.

Well-being was my reward and also wisdom. I grew and I had joy from my growth from word to word I was led to word, from one act to another.

Like Wodan, Odin is also known, how he sacrificed an eye and became all-seeing and all-knowing precisely because of it.

God of battle and war

Odin is a warrior in many ways. Especially with words. The art of words was highly regarded in Nordic civilization. There was a pervasive culture of debate, (where the loser could literally lose his head...). In fact and in principle, Wodan is not a deity of war; our ancestors invoked him in their defensive battle against Roman aggressors: Wodan was, is and remains the God of Love. Never did he incite men to war; man has always done that himself (and usually blamed Wodan/God).

However, when he went to war, he appeared terrifying in the eyes of his enemies. This was because he understood the art of changing his appearance and form in many ways to suit his fancy. Also, he could speak so smoothly and well that anyone listening to him thought that alone was the truth. He said everything in verse, as is still done in poetry today. He and his priests were called "verse makers," because they started that art in the Nordic countries (*Prose Edda, Gylfaginning, 8)*.

Odin is related to other Indo-European gods such as Indra and Zeus. But among the ancient Nordic peoples there was no real priesthood, so the rank or caste of nobles (and warriors) was the highest. Therefore, their supreme god would also serve as god of war and that role was not for a subordinate like Mars with the Romans. According to Georges Dumézil, war colored and encapsulated everything in ideology and practices of the Germanic people.

Odin was held in particularly high esteem by the Vikings, and his worship peaked in the 8th and 9th centuries. Rugged sailors and marauders were attracted to "the father of the fallen," who housed the Einherjar ("glorious dead") in Valhalla.

During this period, the one-eyed Odin presumably replaced Týr, the sky god of the northern European peoples according to the Romans. Tyr, too, was a god of war, but Odin animated the most fanatical warriors. He could put men into a state of frenzy, so that they feared nothing and felt no pain.

Odin could work that his enemies in battle became blind, deaf, or filled with fear, and that their weapons became as sharp as brooms. His men fought without armor and behaved like mad dogs or wolves, bit their shields, were strong as bears or bulls. They killed people, and neither fire nor iron could harm them. Such a thing is called berserker rage (*Prose Edda, Gylfaginning*, 9).

These terrifying "berserkers" plunged into battle naked and with loud noise, the body painted completely black. They were a terror to the Romans. Odin's name means as much as "frenzy" or "madness," suggesting a similar possession to that of the Irish hero Cú Chulainn. The fact that Odin became chief god shows how important warfare had become for the Germanic people. Odin, by the way, did not embody combativeness: he merely instilled it in others.Odin is always sowing conflict and once ordered Freyja to have two princes at each other's throats, so that their vassals had to wade through pools of blood on the battlefield.Gathering fallen warriors in Valhalla is the only strategy he can follow in view of the gods' twilight. He desperately needs the Einherjar, warriors in word and deed, for the final battle against the frost giants on the Vigrid Plain, which almost no one will survive.During the gods' twilight, even Odin is killed by the all-consuming wolf Fenrir, one of Loki's children. The god of creation goes down with his creation.

God of magic and medicine

Odin is simultaneously the god of wisdom and sorcery (knowledge and skill). He is almost all for wisdom. So much so that he had cast his one eye into the well of Mimir in exchange for wisdom. He received initial deep wisdom by hanging himself for nine days on the world tree Yggdrasil. Through this voluntary death and subsequent resurrection (his self-imposed initiation as the first shaman) he obtained greater wisdom than anyone else. The *Gylfaginning* tells the following about him:

- Ódin could change shape. Then his body would lie there as if dead or asleep, and in the meantime he would be a bird or a four-footed animal or a fish or a snake, and so he would go at lightning speed to distant lands to attend to his affairs or those of others. He could also by words alone quench fire, calm the sea and make the wind blow from any direction he pleased.
- Ódin had a ship called *Skíðblaðnir*, with which he sailed great seas; that ship could be folded up like a cloth.
- Òdin always had the head of Mímír with him, which told him much news from other worlds. Sometimes he raised the dead from the earth or sat among those who were hanged. That is why he was also called Lord of the Dead or Lord of the Hanged. He owned two ravens that he had learned to speak. They flew all over the world and brought him many messages. Through all this he became extremely wise. All these arts he taught in runes and songs called `magic songs'. This is why the Æsir are also called `wizards'.
- Ódin mastered the art that gives the most power, the `seidr,' and practiced it himself. This allowed him to know the fate of people

105

and the future. He could also cause death, misfortune or illness of people and rob them of their minds or power and give it to others. When this kind of ritual took place, it was accompanied by so much sexual indulgence that it was felt that men could not lead such rituals without disgrace, and therefore this art was taught to priestesses.

- Óðin always knew where money was hidden in the ground and knew the spells by which the earth, the mountains, the rocks and burial mounds opened up to him, and with words alone he bound those who were to look after the treasures, went in and took what he wanted.
- The people made offerings to Óðin and to the other eleven princes and they called them their gods and for a long time they believed in them.
- Because of these powers, he became very famous. His enemies feared him, but his friends trusted him and believed in him and in his power. He taught most of his arts to his priests. They were almost as wise and skilled in magic as himself. However, many others learned a great deal from them as well, and so the magic arts spread far and wide and continued for a long time.
- From Óðin's name the name Auðun was derived. The people gave that name to their sons, just as they used the name of Thór in such names as Thórir, Thórarin, Steinthór and Hafthór.

Odin further allows himself to be kept abreast of the developing knowledge and events in the nine worlds by sending his two faithful ravens out and having them come and report back to him.

Runes

As mentioned earlier, Odin hung himself on the tree of life to nurture his wisdom. One of those things was obtaining the magical runes (*zipping* the *runes*). These signs consist of powerful lines. This with purpose to draw them easily on rocks, metals or wood. The runes were said to give access to the powerful forces of nature.

- His ring Draupnir both forged by the dwarves. The ring produces nine golden rings every nine days.
- The ravens Huginn (thought) and Muninn (memory) sit on his shoulders. They fly around the world and tell Odin everything they learn during their travels.

- He often carries a cup in his hand, symbol of the cosmos (the cauldron), from which he drinks the mead called Oddroerir, which ferments his spirit and bubbles up wisdom and new knowledge.
- Odin walks around with a staff whose bud constantly bears fresh green leaves and flowers.
- Following Odin are the wolves Geri (gluttony, greed) and Freki (gluttony, avarice) whom he feeds. He himself does not eat, but only drinks the wine.

Odin is also associated with the concept of the Wild Hunt, a noisy, roaring horde, moving through space at the head of the defeated (directly comparable to the Vedic Rudra and the Maruts).

Odin shares the festival of Joel (Dec. 21) with the god Ull.

Odin in the Prologue of the Prose-Edda

According to the Prologue of the Prose-Edda, Voden (Odin) descended from Tror (Thor) after seventeen generations (Loridi, Einridi, Vingethor, Vingenir, Moda, Magi, Seskef, Bedvig, Athra-Annar, Itrmann, Heremod, Skjaldun-Skjold, Biaf-Bjar, Jat, Gudolf, Finn, Friallaf-Fridleif). Thor is said to be the son of Munon (Mennon) and Troan, the daughter of Priamus of Troy. Thor grew up in Thrace (Trudheim) with Count Loricus and his wife Lora (Glora). Odin decided to leave Turkey in Asia (the Far and Middle East were considered parts of Asia) and traveled north to Saxland, Reidgotaland and Sweden, where he met King Gylfi. Odin's son Veggdegg ruled East Saxland, his second son Beldegg (Baldr) ruled Westphalia, and the descendants of his third son Siggi (Sigi), the Völsungen, were to rule France. Another son of Odin, Skjold, became king of Reigotaland, and from the Skjoldungen came the family of Danish kings. In Sweden, Odin founded Sigtun (near Stockholm). In Norway, Odin's son Saeming became king, progenitor of the Norse kings. Yngvi succeeded his father Odin as a king of Sweden. He was the progenitor of the Ynglingen.

Religious customs

People worshipped the Nordic gods in various ways. Large statues of Thor, Odin and Freyr stood in the impressive temple at Uppsala in Sweden, where human sacrifices were also made, among other things. In the smaller temples, priests brought service offerings, especially to Thor and Freyr.

People also paid their respects in less dramatic ways: they offered sacrifices to sacred woods, rocks or stones that they saw as the abode of patron gods or goddesses. This type of sacrifice usually consisted of food.

They also built simple altars of piled stones in the open air. The temples were often very simple.

People also chose natural holy places, such as Helgafell (Holy Mountain) in Iceland. Thorolf Mostur-Beard, a devout follower of Thor, said that this mountain was so sacred that no one could look at it unwashed and no living creature would be harmed there. The same Thorolf also followed a widespread custom by throwing the wooden struts of his high chair overboard as his ship approached Ireland. This allowed Thor to guide him to the place that would be his home.

Thorolf regarded this place designated by Thor as sacred and no one was allowed to desecrate it with blood.

- Bolverk (mischief maker)
- Har (the very tall one), Herran (Herjan, lord)
- Harbard (graybeard)
- Jafnhar (equal high)
- Thidi (the third)
- Vegtam (the road expert)
- Helafell (holy mountain)
- Uppsala (Temple to Sweden)
- Nikar (Hnikar), Nikuz (Hnikud)
- Fjolnir (wise one)
- Oski (fulfiller of desire)
- Omi
- Biflidi (Biflindi) (spear driller)
- Svidar, Svidrir, Vidrir (ruler of weather)
- Jalg (Jalk)
- Fimbultyr (powerful god), wanted Niflheim and Muspelheim created

Ragnarok

In Nordic mythology, **Ragnarök** or **Ragnarok** means the "*fate of the ruling powers*," which has historically been reduced to the meaning of "downfall of the gods (and the world). This would take place in the form of a final battle between unleashed giants and gods, in which the fire giant Surt lights the fuse and destroys just about everything with his flaming sword. Prior to that, most of the gods, giants and monsters have already perished in this cosmic battle.

But Ragnarok is at once an end point and a beginning point. After the battle, the world will be ravaged by natural disasters and eventually disappear into the sea, after which the world will once again emerge fresh green above the waves. The gods will be reborn and the world will be repopulated by two surviving humans.

Name meanings

One must distinguish between Ragnarök (or Ragnarok) and Ragnarokr (with end-r), as there is a subtle difference in meaning:

- **Ragnarök**: (Old Norse "*fates of the powers*"; from *regin*, gen. pl. *ragna* = ruling power (god) + *rök* = cause, sense of origin, turn of events, as still colloquially *have 'den raak'*: to be touched by fate). The term *Ragnarök* indicates how ruling powers fare from beginning to end. So the laws to which their rise, development and disappearance seem to conform. One speaks here of the history and downfall of the gods, as set forth in the Völuspá.

- **Ragnarøkkr** or *Ragnarøkr (Old Norse meaning "*downfall of the powers*"; from *regin*, gen. pl. *ragna* = ruling power (god) + røkkr = darkness, hence extinction, eclipse, downfall). This term arose on the basis of a misinterpretation by Snorri Sturluson of the Völuspá, who in his rendering of the Prose Edda writes *ragna rökr* every time. This magnified only this facet of the original concept, namely the downfall of the gods. Based on Snorri's work, this facet was then further elaborated as "Götterdämmerung."

This is not even just about the "gods," but as much about the Æsir as the Giants and other mythical creatures.

So their fate becomes their downfall.

It appears that further and further departed from the original mythological concept. To what extent this occurred under the influence of Christianity has not yet been clarified. What is clear, however, is that Snorri exercised some caution in the face of the new Christianized power and changed public opinion.

This is not a struggle between good and evil, as in the Christian sense, but a much greater struggle, that between order and chaos, which merge into one another. Chaos overcomes cosmos to pass into a new order of creation.

Factors of divine destiny

1. A trio of powerful unbeings have emerged as descendants of Loki and Angrboða as a result of how the gods try to restrain them, namely Jörmungandr, Fenrir and Hel.
2. The death of Baldr and the binding of Loki.
3. Fimbulvetr The winter of winters.

These are elements that play into how the fate of the powers develops from beginning to end. It will finally lead to the giants resuming their full power in order to destroy back all the order the gods had established.

The War of the Gods

The first war in the world was that between the two families of gods, the Æsir and the Vanen. This one had a cause: the Æsir mistreated Gullveig (aka Goudroes), who brought gold to the people. However, the Æsir did not manage to eliminate Goudroes, she possessed magical Vanen power. It is likely that Goudroes and the Shining meant one and the same goddess, namely Freya. More importantly, however, the great castle of the Æsir was destroyed by the Vans, because the Æsir did not want to grant the requests of the Vans. The Vans were incestuous and thus engaged in practices pernicious to the Æsir, and therefore the Æsir refused to comply with the Vans' request to distribute the riches of the earth. This as compensation for the mistreatment of Goudroes. War breaks out, the castle, still built by Ask and Embla, is crushed.

Oaths

The peace was signed, the Æsir sent Honir and Mimir to the Vanen, the Vanen sent Freyr, Njord and Freya to the Æsir to ratify the peace.

There is another side to this part of the story: Mimir (Mijmeraar) was beheaded and the head returned to the Æsir.

But more important now is that a giant, a hrimthurs, has offered to rebuild Asgard, on the condition that he will have Freya as his wife. The Æsir agree to this, provided the fortress will be finished within six months. The giant thus begins building, and to the Æsir's dismay, the entire castle is completed three days before time, with only the gate missing.

Loki invents a ruse, however. The giant builds the fortress with the help of a stallion, and Loki lures the stallion away by turning himself into a mare. When the giant realizes that Loki was behind this, he becomes furious. Then Thor is called in.Without hesitation, he knocks the giant down, ignorant of the whole affair. With a blow from Mjolnir, he beats the giant to death. But the Æsir have now broken their oath, something unforgivable in Nordic culture, and this became a construction defect that resulted in the end of the world.

Fate, Balder's death

That the world would perish had been certain since the creation of the first beings, in the ancient world of ice, void and fire. Yet with the breaking of their oath, the gods involved themselves in this fate, and Balder's death sealed it.

Indeed, a second event that causes the end times is the murder of Baldr, son of Odin and Frigg, a being of light, innocence and perfection. The mother wanted to make the child quasi invulnerable. So there was a vulnerability, (which also brought down heroes like Achilles and Siegfried). She had asked all creatures, trees and plants the promise, never to harm her son. But she had forgotten the mistletoe, a weak wood. Loki seeks out the fragile spot, disguised as an old woman, who elicits Frigg's knowledge of it. He uses Baldr's blind brother Hodr as an instrument and gets him to shoot a mistletoe arrow by helping him aim.

Baldr cannot go to Valhöll because he did not die honorably on the battlefield, so he must go to Hel (the "ordinary" underworld).

Frigg begs everything in the world to let Baldr come back to the world again so that he can then go to Valhöll. Hel's condition is that then everyone on earth must grieve. But there is a giant who refuses to grieve, at Loki's instigation.

But Balder's death would result in a new world being created, after the downfall. Perhaps that also played into Loki's hands, when he had Balder killed by having the blind Hodr shoot the mistletoe arrow at his invincible brother so to speak for the game, with Loki helping him aim.

After the ragnarök, Balder would rise again, and become the captain of the new world. Whereas Loki was seen as Terminator (he was fire god, and the earth would be burned by Surt's flaming sword), Balder may be seen as Beginner, and perhaps the similarities between Jesus and Balder led to a faster acceptance of Christianity. Balder, too, would be resurrected.

The scenario

Ragnarok will be preceded by Fimbulvetr. Three consecutive winters without a summer in between lead to all morality disappearing and conflicts and feuds breaking out.

Finally, the wolf Sköll or Skalli, and his brother Hati will devour Sól (the Sun) and her brother Mani (the Moon), after hunting them for centuries. The stars disappear from the firmament and the world is enveloped in complete darkness.

In the process, the world will shake so violently that all trees will be uprooted, all mountains will collapse, and every tire and shoelace will leap, setting Loki free, and his son the wolf Fenrir will also rid himself of his chains. This terrible wolf's drooling maw will gape so wide that his lower jaw scrapes the ground and his upper jaw the sky. And if there is room for it, he will yawn even wider. Flames dance in his eyes and come out of his nostrils.

As the land floods, the ship hits Naglfar raft, made all along from the finger and toe nails of the dead.The Midgaard snake rises from the deep ocean floor on land and shaking and rooting makes the seas swamp it. With every breath she emits venom, searing earth and air in venom.

Eggther, watchman of the Jötuns will sit on his grave opening strumming his harp, with a grim smile. The red rooster Fjalar will crow to the giants and the golden rooster Gullinkambi will crow to the gods. A third rooster, rust red will raise the dead in the abode of Hel.

Through all that tumult, Muspell's sons come running forward, with Surt in the lead. They attempt to cross the bridge Bifröst, but it collapses as a result. Garm, the hellhound who lay bound for Gnipahellir also comes loose. Thereupon they move to the Vigrid plain and encounter the Fenriswolf, the Midgaardsnake, Loki, Hrym (the helmsman of Naglfar), all the Hrimthursen (riding giants) and Hels retinue. They set up in battle position there.

Then Heimdall rises, with all his strength he blows the Gjallar horn so loudly that it is heard by all nine worlds. All the gods are awakened and immediately gather in deliberation. Odin rides on Sleipnir to Mimir's well for counsel.

Thereupon, Yggdrasil, the world tree (of which the Milky Way forms the upper branches), from root to crown top goes feverishly roaring. Everything on earth, in heaven and in hell goes shaking.

Final battle

The Æsir and all the Einherjar (the fallen heroes from Valhöll in the battle) arm themselves for battle. Odin rides in front with his spear Gungnir, his golden helmet and magnificent armor, followed by this army of 432,000 heroes (800 from each of the 540 gates of Valhöll)).

In the ensuing battle, Freyr fights Surtr, with Freyr losing because (in another myth) he gave away his sword to Skirnir. Garm, the hellhound seizes Tyr and Tyr kills him, but is so wounded in the process that he only lives until after the world is destroyed by fire.Thor manages to kill the

Midgaard serpent with his hammer Mjolnir, but barely nine paces away from the serpent he dies of its venom.

Odin fights Fenrir with his lance for a long time, but is finally swallowed by the wolf. Thereupon Vidar puts his foot on the lower jaw with the sole of his shoe made of saved leather and tears away the upper jaw with his hand, killing Fenrir.Loki fights Heimdall and the two also defeat each other.

Finally, Surt spreads fire across the nine worlds, destroying everything in a comprehensive world fire. The earth structure eventually sinks completely into the primordial ocean.

But the balance between order and chaos is then restored, so that alfather Fimbultyr can allow a whole new world to emerge.In it, Thor's sons Magni and Modi meet with Odin's son Vidar and Vali a new heaven corresponding to the former Asgard. Baldr and Hödr return from the realm of Hel.

After Ragnarok

Grain will ripen on the fields that were never sown. The meadow Idavoll, on the site of the now destroyed Asgaard, was spared. The sun resurfaces as Sol before being swallowed again by Sköll, as she gives birth to a daughter, as beautiful and strong as herself. That daughter will continue her path across the sky.

A few gods survive the test of fire: Odin's brother Vili, Odin's sons Vidar and Vali, Thor's sons Móði and Magni, who inherit their father's magic hammer, and Hœnir, who will swing the staff and foretell what must happen. Baldr and his brother Hodr, who died before the Ragnarok, will return from the former abode of Hel and reside in their father Odin's former hall, Valhalla in heaven. At their meeting on Idavoll, these gods will then sit together and discuss their hidden knowledge, including the ailments Jörmungandr and Fenrir. In the swaying grass they will find the golden chess games that belonged to the Æsir and look at them in wonder. (Of the goddesses, none was explicitly mentioned, but there are assumptions that Frigg, Freya and most of the other Vanir will survive).

Two people will also escape the final destruction of the world by hiding deep inside Yggdrasil, where Surtr's sword cannot destroy. They are Lif and Lifthrasir (*Life* and *Livelihood*). When they appear from their hiding place, they live on morning dew and repopulate the human world. They will honor their new pantheon, led by Baldr.

There will be many halls left to house the souls of the departed. According to the Prose-Edda, there exists another heaven south of Asgard, called Andlang, and a third even further above it, called Vidblain. These are spaces sheltered from Surtrs fire. According to both Edda, the best place after the Ragnarok is Gimle, a building more beautiful than the sun, with golden roof, in the sky. There the gods live in peace with themselves and with each other. There will be a hall Brimir, a hall on Okolnir ("*never cold*"), where many good drinks are served. And then there will be Sindr, an excellent hall space, made entirely of red gold on Nidafjoll ('the dark mountains'). In it will dwell the souls of the righteous.

Finally, the Prose Edda mentions Náströnd ("*body beach*" or *corpse beach*). An equally wide and unfavorable place in the underworld, where no sunlight penetrates, with all doors facing north, walls and roofs made of braided serpents, with their heads inward, spewing so much poison that it flows through them like rivers. That is the place through which oathbreakers, murderers and professional flirters must wade forever.

And in the worst place of all, Hvergelmir, the cosmic Noisy Cauldron, the dragon Nidhoggr - another surviving power of the Ragnarok - will do the devil to the bodies of the dead by sucking their blood.

The whole story, however, is not the account of a final end in a so-called "final crack," but the reflection of an optimistic view of the cyclical course of things. After each cycle, a purge has happened, and with the knowledge and experience generated, a new cosmic "attempt" is made with what essentially always remains.

Ratatoskr

In Nordic mythology, **Ratatosk** is the squirrel who conveys messages between the eagle Vidofnir, who sits high in the tree Yggdrasil, and the dragon Nidhogg, who gnaws at the roots of the tree. Ratatosk runs back and forth between the two to convey curses toward each other. Grímnismál mentions him in verse 32.

Originally, Ratatosk was seen as the messenger. Later descriptions added that he also twisted the messages of Nidhogg and the Eagle, thus sowing discord between the two bantams. His nickname then also became the "Twist Sower.

Sif

Goddess of harvest and land

Sif (meaning: *Sibbe*) in Nordic mythology is the Asin of agriculture and fertility. She is daughter of Odin and wife of Thor.

Together they had a daughter Thrud ("strength") and a son Modi. The fast bowman Ullr, son from a previous relationship, brought them into the marriage.

The golden hair probably represents the mature corn.

Sigi

The ancestor of the Volsung lineage

In Nordic mythology, **Sigi** is the grandfather of Völsung, the progenitor of the famous Völsung lineage, to which Sigmund and his son Sigurd belonged. Sigi, according to the Völsunga saga, is the son of Odin and the father of Rerir. He was killed by his brothers-in-law.

In the prologue of the Prose Edda, it is mentioned that he ruled Frakland (the land of the Franks). And his name falls in the Nafnapulur, the last part of the Skáldskaparmál of the same Proza Edda. The Völsunga saga mentions Hunaland, which refers to both the territories of the Franks (*Hugones* in Latin, *Hugas* in Old English) and the Huns.

Sigi, one of Odin's sons, killed the slave Bredi during a deer hunt because he had put down more animals than he had. Sigi buried Bredi in a snow mountain, but still the murder came true and he had to leave the land. Odin gave him a ship and companions out of pity, and Sigi ruled the Hun kingdom elsewhere, until he was killed by his wife's brothers. When he returned from a distant journey, his son Rerir discovered what had happened, took revenge and became the new ruler.

Sigi

Sigyn

Also spelled Siguna.

Goddess of earth

Sigyn or *Sigunn*, in Nordic mythology, is the wife of the Æsir god Loki, who bore him two sons, Narfi and Vali.

Finally, when Loki was tied to three rocks by the Æsir to keep him from further misdeeds after murdering Baldr, it was she who tried to ease his suffering. Instead of abandoning him, she went with a cup to catch the biting venom that dripped from Jormungandr onto him. Each time the bowl was full Sigyn had to leave him for a moment to go and empty it and then the venom dripped into his eyes.

According to certain sources, the meaning of her name is "Victory giver.

Sleipnir

Sleipnir is an eight-legged stallion from Nordic mythology, immensely strong and the fastest horse in existence. He is Odin's horse and, according to tradition, carried him through the heavens and into the underworld. Sleipnir is the child of Loki and Svadilfari. Sleipnir is said to have made Iceland during his first footstep here on earth.

Sleipnir would later also have killed his "sister" Hel, but is eaten during Ragnarok (end of times) by his "brother" Fenrir, the giant wolf. All Loki's children have one thing in common, they are monsters; although Sleipnir is the only good creature.Odin would also later win Sleipnir during a race with a giant.

Birth of Sleipnir

When the thunder god Thor was destroying giants in the north, a disguised frost giant came to offer himself in Asgaard. On condition that he be given the sun and moon and be allowed to make Freya his wife, he would restore the destroyed walls of Asgaard in six months. The gods agreed, assuming that this giant could never accomplish that arduous task in such a short time. In doing so, the frost giant did ask if he could use his horse, Svadilfari, for this purpose. Loki was the one who agreed to this, even before the other gods could answer.

When the giant had almost finished the fortress until three days before time - he only had to add the gate - the gods were furious with Loki. After all, they would lose the sun, the moon and Freya, and wanted to torture Loki forever. Loki, however, devised a ruse. He transformed himself into a white mare and lured Svadilfari away from the frost giant. This made the latter so angry that he immediately began to tear down the walls of Asgaard again. At this moment Thor returned and beat the giant to death with his hammer Mjölnir.

Later, Loki gave birth to Sleipnir, the descendant of both Loki and the horse Svadilfari.

Sol and Mani

Personification of the sun and moon

Sól is counted among the Asinnen. This Sun Goddess from Nordic mythology, like her brother the Moon God (Máni), is pursued by wolves. Sól rode every day on her chariot pulled by the two horses Arvak and Alsvid. She was pursued by the wolf Sköll, who wanted to devour her. During a solar eclipse, it was thought that Sól was almost eaten by Sköll. Sól would eventually be swallowed, but her place would then be taken by her daughter.

The sun itself was called Alfrodull, which means as much as "Alfenrad." In Norse belief, the sun itself did not give light; this was given by the moons Alsvid and Arvak.

The Old Norse name *Sól* means "sun." In Germanic mythology, the second Merseburg spell mentioned *Sunna* (Old High German for "sun"). In addition, she is also known as *Sunne*. Her Anglo-Saxon name is *Sigel*.

Sól is the daughter of the giantess Mundilfari who was married to Glaur. She was married to Glenr.

The earth is protected from the sun's heat by Swalin who stood between Sól and the earth like a shield.

Máni

Máni is the personification of the moon in Nordic mythology. The Old Norse word *máni* simply means "moon."

In the Vafþrúðnismál and in the Gylfaginning, Mundilfari is his father and Sól, the sun, is his sister. Snorri Sturluson tells in the Gylfaginning that the wolf Hati chases the moon across the sky and finally devours it. The wolf Sköll will then devour the sun (Sól).

Surtr

Surt (Old Norse *surthr* "the black one"; also *Surtr, Surtur*), in Nordic mythology, is the fire giant who lives in Muspelheim. He guards the entrance to this world of fire with the flaming sword Surtalogi, which will later set the world ablaze. His wife's name is Sinmore. Surt is sometimes considered the son of Svart and is enemy number one of the Ashes.

In the Old Norse creation story, Muspel is mentioned as ruler of Muspelheim; probably they are identical. In the Ragnarök, he divides with his fire sword the bridge Bifröst, the connection between Midgard and Asgard. With the sons of Muspel (the *Surts*), he sets fire to the world, hurling fire in all directions and destroying all life (World Fire). He then also kills the unarmed Freyr, god of fertility and life, in a duel.

The known texts never speak of his origins. He seems to have always been there. The flames, on the other hand, are at the origin of creation, for when the fire of Muspelheim met the mists of Niflheim, they provided the genesis of the hermaphrodite Ymir and the primordial cow Audhumla.

Svartalfer

In Nordic mythology, the **svartalfer** (black elves, usually translated as night elves) are the counterparts of the light elves. The light elves live in Alfheim, the svartalfer in Svartalfheim.

According to Nordic mythology, *svartalfer* are evil. They look like humans, but are as black as night.

The svartalfer are often confused with the dwarves, and their realm with the realm of the dwarves, Nidavellir. Yet there are distinct differences. For example, dwarves - unlike night elves - are generally benign. Also, dwarves live in Nidavellir, not in Svartalfheim.In English folklore, night elves were called "goblins," which translates as earthman. After the Christianization of the Vikings, with which their mythology also fell into oblivion, the English goblin continued to exist, but his malevolence waned over time, until he became just an annoying prankster.

Svaðilfari

Svadilfari (meaning "Unlucky Traveler") is a giant horse from Nordic mythology that could work like no other. It is also the father of Sleipnir.

One day the gods decided that the Asgard should be protected by a wall. However, they themselves had no desire to begin this enormous work. Then a giant presented himself who was willing to do the work. He proposed to complete the work in three half years, but in return the gods had to give him Freya, the goddess of love, as a wife.

The gods first thought this was an outrageous proposal (they were fond of their goddess of love) but finally decided to let the giant do the work on the advice of Loki. The latter suggested that the giant start the work but since three half years would be far too little they could get rid of the giant after that time and they would only have to finish part of the wall themselves.

This, however, was beyond the giant's horse. Svadilfari proved so strong that the work progressed at a tremendous pace. Since the gods did not want to lose "their" Freya, a plan had to be devised. Loki provided salvation and turned himself into a mare. At night he lured Svadilfari away that way and deprived him of his sleep.

During the day, the stallion was so tired that he worked a lot slower. So in this way, the giant failed to complete the work within the specified time and the gods got rid of him.

However, the mare Loki was pregnant with Svadilfari and Wodan forbade Loki to resume his normal form and ordered him to complete his gestation and bring the foal into the world. This foal became Wodan's famous eight-legged stallion Sleipnir.

Tanngrisnir and Tanngnjóstr

In Nordic mythology, **Tandgniostr** and **Tandgrisnir** (*teeth grinder* and *teeth grinder*, also called **Tanngnjóstr** and **Tanngrisnir**) are the two goats or bucks that pull Thor's chariot.

Thor can eat the goats and then puts the bones back in their skin. With Mjölnir, he brings the magical animals back to life the next morning so they can pull the chariot again.

In *Thor and Loki in Jotunheim,* the goats are slaughtered by Thor. He brings them back to life the next day, but one of the goats turns out to be paralyzed. Through a ruse by Loki, Thialfi has sucked the marrow from a bone. The farmer then gives his children Thialfi and Röskwa as atonement as servants to Thor.

Thor

Also spelled Thorr, Thunor, Thonar, Donar, Donner, Thur, Thunar, or Thunaer.

God of strength, protection, war, storms, thunder and, lightning

Thor (runic: þonar ᚦᚢᚾᚨᚱ), in Continental Germanic mythology **Donar**, in Old Norse Þórr, in Old Saxon **Thunaer** or **Thunar,** and also known as Stavo is the thunder god in Nordic and Germanic mythology. He was a son of Odin and the earth goddess Fjorgyn.

As a child, he was strong and, in addition, difficult to raise. Therefore, he was raised by two lightning spirits, Vingnir and Hlora. He grew into a huge man, almost a giant, with equal strength, and his hammer Mjölnir made him even stronger.

Thor befriended Loki and his favorite pastime was slaying giants. He represents order in the face of chaos.

Stories

These two traits are both reflected in Þrýmskviða, in which the giant Þrymr steals Thor's hammer. Þrymr is only willing to give it back if he gets Freya, the fertility goddess, as his wife. This of course is impossible, without Freya, summer would never set in (the Teutons knew only summer and

127

winter), and so Loki forged a plan. He borrowed Freya's feather dress and had Thor put it on. Dressed as a woman, Thor, together with Loki, went to Útgard, in the land of the Jötun, where they were warmly received by Þrymr, for the latter thought that Thor was Freya; so that part of the plan succeeded. But Thor ate and drank so much that the giants noticed. Loki, however, explained that Freya was so pleased to be married to the famous Þrymr that she had not eaten for seven days and seven nights. Shortly thereafter, when the giants were drunk enough, he asked to give the hammer and thereupon Thor struck all the giants present dead.

Tyr tells Thor about Hymir's cauldron and they meet Tyr's grandmother with nine hundred heads. Both are first hidden by the woman when Hymir comes home and a feast follows. Thor eats two bulls. However, he must provide food the next day and captures a dragon (or snake), the Midgaard snake Jormungandr, with the head of an ox. Then Thor must break a cup, but fails. Following the woman's advice, he throws the cup against the giant's head, whereupon the object breaks. Thor, together with Tyr, takes the cauldron home.

Also in the Hymiskviða, another Edda song, are some strong stories about Thor. There, too, he makes himself known as an excessive eater. Perhaps he has this trait to show that in fact he himself is not inferior to the giants, who are Jötnar (eaters) and Thursten (drinkers) of all that is available. In Thor and Loki in Jotunheim, Thor and Loki are given impossible tasks.

In Alvíssmál, a dwarf (Alvis, aka Alwis) gets engaged to Þrúðr (Thor's daughter). When Thor returns home after eight months, he does not find this a suitable mate for her. He decides to ask the dwarf questions and the dwarf answers them. Then the sun rises and the dwarf petrifies.

Wodan (as the ferryman Hairbeard or Greybeard) meets Thor when he wants to cross the river. Hairbeard is only allowed to ferry honest souls across on the boat of Battle Wolf. Thor claims to be the son of Wodan, to have killed the giant Berggevaarte and to have won many other battles. Wodan tells of his adventures with women. After a long discussion full of ridicule, he continues to refuse to take Thor across the river.

Thor's Mjolnir

Thor's magic hammer

Mjölnir, **Mjöllnir** or **Mjollnir** in Nordic mythology is the warhammer of Thor, the god of thunder. The hammer was crafted for him by the dwarves Brokkr and Eitri, who made magical objects for the gods. The meaning of the name is controversial and ranges from "pulverizer" to "thunderbolt."

Features

It was said of Mjölnir that he never missed his target and, when thrown, returned to Thor's right hand to which he wore an iron glove. The hammer was also said to be so heavy that only Thor himself could lift it. By quickly swinging the hammer around, releasing it and grabbing it at the last moment, Thor could "fly" and thus move over great distances, including back and forth to Asgard, the realm of the Norse Gods. Because of Thor, who was also the protector of marriage, Mjölnir was also seen as the symbol of marriage, and even as an erotic symbol.

Mjollnir was greatly feared by the ice giants, the enemies of the gods, because Thor had destroyed many ice giants with it, including the great giant Hrungnir.

The power of the Mjölnir was known and feared even by the giants of the Utgard, for Thor had struck three deep valleys in their land with growing wrath, thinking he was punishing the insolent giant Skrymir.

According to the Eddal song Þrymskviða, Mjölnir was once stolen by the giant Þrymr, who demanded marriage to the goddess Freya as compensation for the hammer. Thor thereupon disguised himself as Freya, and Loki as his servant. Twice Þrymr almost discovered that he had been tricked, but finally he sent for Mjölnir, whereupon Thor killed the giant and his retinue.

According to popular belief, it thundered and lightned every time Thor threw his hammer. The hammer was meant to be one of three perfect gifts for the gods, but the handle of the hammer was said to be one inch too short, because Loki disguised as a hornet stabbed the dwarf Brokkr in the forehead during its manufacture.

Origin

The motif of Mjölnir as the causer of lightning occurs throughout northern Europe, that is, among the Celts, Teutons, Balts and Slavs. For example, the word *Mjölnir* is related to Old Norse *myln* "fire," Welsh *mellt*, *mellen* "lightning," Old Prussian *mealde* "lightning" and Russian *mólnija* "lightning. Latvian has the word *milna* 'hammer of the thunder god Perkuns,' which agrees well with Mjölnir in both form and meaning. Indo-Europeanists therefore assume that the various words go back to a single primal form, namely *meld^{h}nio- or *mld^{h}nieh$_2$-. The same is true of the associated thunder gods, with the underlying hypothetical Indo-European thunder god Perkwunos.

The name *Mjölnir* has also been interpreted folk etymologically as "grinder" in the sense of "grinding stone," in that it totally pulverizes that against which it is turned.

Symbolism

Mjölnir was simultaneously worn around the neck as an amulet to symbolize Thor (see image). Several forms of hammer amulets existed (and still exist), such as the *Schonen Hammer*.

From the transition time from paganism to Christianity, amulets were found in Scandinavia, which could possibly be seen as either a cross or a Thor hammer.In those transition times, the Thor amulet (the Thor hammer) was publicly seen as a sign of adherence to the ancient faith.

Týr

God of war, justice in battle, victory and, heroic glory

Týr (pronounced *tuur*) is the god of justice in Nordic mythology. He is the son of Odin and Frigg.

Name

The Old Norse name *Týr* is a continuation of the Primal Germanic (reconstructed) word **Tīwaz*. In Old English it was called *Tīw* or *Tīg*.

Germanic names for Tuesdays are often derived from the names of this god.

Kinship

Týr is apparently somewhat outside the family relationships of the Old Norse gods.A wife is almost nowhere mentioned in the Old Norse literature and there is ambiguity about his father.

Features

Týr is the god behind the similarly named rune, or rune *T* (an arrow pointing upward). The rune *T* belongs to Týr and represents justice, discipline, self-sacrifice and it is a warrior rune.

Týr is the sky father and personifies the sun. In addition, as god of the sword and spear, Týr is also the god of war. Týr provides justice, honor, courage and wisdom in battle. Since Týr provides justice, he is also the god of the "thing" (the Germanic people's assembly).

Týr was one of the main Germanic gods around the beginning of our era, being compared to Zeus in Greek mythology. Later -in the time of the Vikings- he faded somewhat into the background. Odin became the most popular and thus the most important god. At the end of time (Ragnarok), Týr will kill the hellhound Garmr.

Since Týr was once such an important god, it is likely that he is the continuation of an older Indo-Germanic deity. However, the connection with the deity names Zeus and Dyaus and words such as Latin 'deus' and French 'dieu' (for 'god') is not so transparent as to speak of an immediate kinship.

Edda

In the Edda, Týr tells Thor about Hymir's cauldron and they meet Tyr's grandmother with nine hundred heads. Both are first hidden by the woman when Hymir comes home and a feast follows. Thor eats two bulls. However, he must provide food the next day and catches a dragon (or snake) with the head of an ox. Then Thor must break a cup, but fails. Following the woman's advice, he throws the cup against the giant's head and then the object breaks. Thor, together with Tyr, takes the cauldron home.

Equivalents

The Greek god Ares, Ziu and Mars.

Saxnôt

The Roman Tacitus, in his *Germania* (c. 98 AD), compared the Germanic gods to the Roman ones. Thus Wodan (Odin) was seen as Mercury

(hence mercredi/wednesday/Wednesday/Wednesday); Donar (Thor) was
compared to Hercules (son of Jupiter) (jeudi/thursday/Thursday) and
Tiwaz (the Saxon Saxnôt) to Mars (mardi/tuesday/Tuesday).

Tyrfing

Tyrfing was a magical sword mentioned in a poem in the Hervarar saga. The name is also used to refer to the Goths, and the name *Tervingi* was used by the Romans in the 4th century.

Svafrlami, grandson of Odin, was king of Gardariki. He managed to capture the dwarves Dvalin and Durin when they left their rock where they lived. He forced them to forge a sword with a golden hilt that would never miss its mark, that would never rust and that cut through stone and iron as easily as through clothes.

The dwarves made this sword, and it sparkled and shone like fire. Out of revenge, however, they cursed the sword so that every time it was drawn someone had to die because of it. It was also said to be the cause of three great evils. The curse also came to mean that the sword would be the cause of the death of Svafrlami himself.

When Svafrlami learned of the curse, he tried to kill Dvalin, but the dwarf disappeared into the rock, and the sword was driven deep into the stones, missing its target.

Svafrlami was killed by the berserker Arngrim, who took the sword from him. After Arngrim, the sword was carried by his sons Angantyr and his eleven brothers. They were all killed at Samsø by the Swedish champion Hjalmar and his Norwegian sworn brother Orvar-Odd. Hjalmar however was wounded by Tyrfing only has time before he dies to sing his death song and ask Orvar-Odd to take his body to Ingeborg in Uppsala.

The daughter of Angantyr and his wife Tofa, Hervor grew up as a serf, knowing nothing of her lineage. When she does learn of her lineage, however, she arms herself as a shield maiden and goes to Munarvoe in Samsø in search of the cursed dwarven sword. Eventually she finds it and after many warrior battles she is tired of the warrior life and marries Hofund. They have two sons: Heidrek and Angantyr. In a quarrel, Heidrek kills his brother Angantyr with a stone. His father Hofund expels him but Hervor secretly gives the sword Tyrfing to her son.

Heidrek became king of the Goths by conquering it from King Harald. With his daughter Helga, he had a son whom he named after his grandfather: Angantyr. He also had another son with Sifka, the daughter of the Hun king Humli: Hlöd and another daughter with Hergerd, the daughter of King Hrollaug: Hervör.During a journey, Heidrek camped near the Carpathians.

He was accompanied by nine servants. While Heidrek was sleeping, however, the servants broke into his tent, took Tyrfing and killed Heidrek. This was the last of Tyrfing's three evil deeds. Heidrek's son, Angantyr caught the slaves, killed them, took the sword and the curse was lifted.

Angantyr became the next king of the Goths, but his illegitimate half- hun brother Hlod (Hlöd, Hlöðr) asked for half the kingdom. Angantyr refused and Gizur reproached Hlod for being a bastard and his mother a slave. Hlod and 343 200 mounted Huns invaded the kingdom. The Huns are far more numerous than the Goths, but the Goths win because Angantyr uses Tyrfing to kill his brother Hlod. The huge amount of corpses clogged the rivers causing a flood that filled the valleys with corpses of both humans and horses.

Ull

Also spelled Ullr.

A god associated with skis and the bow

Ullr (Old Norse, also called Ull, Holler, Oller, Uller or Vulder, Old High German *Wulder*) is in Nordic mythology the eleventh Ase and god of Winter, hunting, dueling, meadows and fields. He is such a good archer and skiloper that no one can compete with him. He is beautiful to behold and an outstanding warrior. It is good to invoke him in a duel fight.

Ullr lives in his self-built hall Ydalir (yew valley)

Researchers suspect it must be a very ancient deity, underscoring its relationship with magic. In many regions, Ullr was worshipped as the main god. (Phillipson, "Die Genealogie der Götter")

He shows up in later times in the Edda as Sif's son and Thor's stepson.

In the 20th century, Ullr was rediscovered and thus carried to this day in medallion form as a talisman by skiers. The medallion is then usually carved from the rose of a deer's or stag's antlers. It is pierced and fastened to the belt by hikers with leather straps.

Snorri's note that a shield can also be called *Ullr's ship* is further supported by connotations such as *askr Ullar*, *far Ullar* and *kjóll Ullar* which all mean *"Ullr's ship"* and refer to shields. The origin of this kenning is not known, but it could be related to Ullr's identity as a ski god. Earlier skis, or skates, would have come from shields. A later Icelandic composition, *Laufás-Edda*, provides the prosaic explanation that Ullr's ship was called *"Skjöldr,"* shield.

Consequently, Ullr's name appears more often in war announcements:

Ullr branding - Ullr of sword - warrior

edge-Ullr - shield-Ullr - warrior

Ullr almsíma - Ullr of bowstring - warrior

Three skalden poems, Þórsdrápa, *Haustlöng* and an excerpt by Eysteinn Valdason, refer to Thor as Ullr's stepfather and confirm Snorri's information.

Útgarðar

Útgard (or Buitenplaats) in Nordic mythology is the utterly rarefied area of Jotenheim, the castle of the Thursen and Joten. It is told of this place that it was dark, and probably cold, for giants petrified at the sight of the sun.

In *Thor and Loki in Jotunheim,* the gods taught that Útgard was a delusion conjured up by the giants to frighten them.

Valhalla

The hall of the fallen warriors

Valhalla (from Old Icelandic *Valhöll*) literally means *Hall (höll, halla) for the Fallen (fall, shore)*.In Nordic mythology, Valhalla was a special heaven reserved for those killed in battle. For the Vikings, being killed in battle was the highest honor a man could achieve.

According to the Vikings, Valhalla was the realm of the god Odin. The Vikings believed that Odin's heroes (einherjar) died daily in battle to be brought from the battlefield to Valhalla in the evening by Odin's warmaids, the Walkuren. Here they were treated to pork (the wild boars Andrimner, Särimner and Eldrimner) and honey wine. Each morning the warriors returned to battle to be killed again.

The Vikings were convinced that Valhalla was a huge hall located in Asgard. Its dimensions were phenomenal. According to the Grimnismál, Valhalla would have 540 halls with 540 gates. From each gate, 800 warriors could attack (432,000 warriors). The walls consisted of spears, the roof was made of shields and on the benches were armor. In front of the western gates hung wolves with an eagle dripping with blood above them. Valhalla was surrounded by the moat Tund (river of fire) and guarded by the werewolf (human wolf) Tjodvitner, who fished for humans in the river. On the roof were a deer, Oak Thorn, and a goat, Heiðrun, and both ate from the tree Læraðr (which is often thought of as the world tree

Yggdrasil). The goat Heiðrun produced the mead that the warriors drank. From the deer's antlers dripped water from Laerad in Hvergelmir, the source of all waters. Some of the fallen also stayed in Vingólf ("friendly house").

Wodan (with the help of the earth woman Strife Joy and the snake Doorbek) retrieved the rejuvenating drink of spring rain to Valhalla after the giants stole it.

Not all the fallen went to Odin, Freya got half of the fallen, they came to Folkvangr (Field of the People).

Besides Valhalla, another realm of the dead existed, Niflhel, which was meant for the sick, the elderly, the women and men who had died a natural death. This world was guided by the goddess Hel. The entrance was guarded by the dog Garmr.

Vali

Also spelled Ali.

God of vengeance

Vali was a son of Odin and destined to avenge Balder's death by killing Hodr.

He went from infant to adult in a day and killed Hodr instantly. With his half-brother Vidar, he would survive the Ragnarok.

This Vali is often confused with another Vali, who was the son of Loki and Sigyn and was the brother of Narfi. This Vali was turned into a drooling wolf who bit Narfi's throat.

Valkyries

Beautiful maidens who choose the heroes to be slain in battle and conduct them to Valhalla

The **Walkuren** (Old Norse *valkyrjar*) are battle goddesses from Nordic mythology. Originally they were grim death and war goddesses, who scoured the battlefields on the backs of hellhounds in search of felled (fallen) heroes to serve as messengers for Odin before the final battle during ragnarok.

Eventually, the Valkyries evolved in popular culture from ugly witches mostly into fair maidens. They were the servants or daughters of Odin and wore beautiful armor with helmets and spears and sat on horses with wings.

Although the Walkurs are frequently seen as goddesses who took up arms themselves, they did not fight themselves. At least there are no known writings describing that Walkurs themselves participated in battle. Their task was to visit the battlefields and choose the most heroic (slain) warrior and take him to Valhalla. Only the bravest warriors were chosen and they enjoyed a good life in Valhalla until the final battle, the ragnarok.

Picking the bravest among the warriors was a futile attempt by Odin to win the final battle. When the Walkuren were not looking for heroes on the battlefield, they also had another task. For example, they served the heroes in Valhalla.

As long as the Walkurs remained virgins, they would remain immortal and invulnerable.The reflection of their armor caused the aurora.

Vanaheimr

Vanaheim (Old Norse *Vanaheimr*) was the realm of the Vanir (fertility gods) or Wanen. They were the oldest branch of the two families of gods in Nordic mythology. The other, younger family branch were the Aesir (battle gods) or Ashes, who lived in Asgard, far away from Vanaheim.

Shortly after creation, the Vanir and the Aesir fought for supremacy. After the Aesir's victory, peace was established by an exchange of a number of gods on both sides. The Vanir sent the sea god Njörðr and his two children Freyr and Freya as well as the sage Kvasir to Asgard. The Aesir sent Hœnir and the sage Mímir to Vanaheim.

Vanir

A race of Norse gods who warred against and later reconciled with the Aesir

The **Wanen**, also called *Vanir* or *Vanen*, are the followers of Vili and Ve in Nordic mythology. They are opposed to the Æsir. Both of these families of gods arose after Odin, Vili and Ve created the world. Odin was not yet satisfied, but his brothers were, who wanted to go around their creation. Thus the two "families of gods" were created.

Later there would be quarrels between the two families because the Æsir wanted to build a wall to protect Asgaard. The Wanen did not want this because it would hinder their free passage. In fact, the Wanen moved around; they did not stay in one place. Thus a war arose between the Æsir and the Wanen.

Periodically, the two families will reconcile and finally create Kvasir to help them keep the peace by acting as an "ombudsman" between the two families.

In addition, the two families will exchange "hostages." Some of the Æsir will live with the Wanen and vice versa. For example, Njord with his daughter Freya and son Freyr would move to the Asgaard and Hœnir, among others, has begun to travel with the Wanen.

Characteristics

The Wanen are fertility gods, gods of the sea and abundance. Where the Æsir were seen as distinctly acting and often warring gods, the Wanen were regarded as rich, wealth-giving, the patterns of fertility, happiness and peace and, along with the Æsir, of unity.

They possess deep knowledge of magical arts and also know the future. It was said that Freya taught the Æsir magic.

They practiced endogamy and even incest, which was forbidden among the Æsir. For example, Freyr and Freyja were children of Njord and his sister (see Nerthus).

Later conflicts with Christians who tried to convert the pagan North often proved intractable because of the cults surrounding these Wans. In those cults, the Nordic tribes had chosen either the Wanen or the Æsir, or sometimes both. In regions where fishing and shipping prevailed, Wanen cults were more often opted for.

Location

The main residence, the homeland, of the Wanen is Vanaheim, one of the three "upper worlds. But in Nordic mythology, the real presence of the gods is seen scattered around the tree of life Yggdrasil, which extends itself across the cosmos (see: Nordic cosmogony).

Delusions or Alves

The Edda provides a possible identification of the Wanen with the elves (Alven or Alfar), as it often mentions "the Æsir and Wanen" as well as "the Æsir and Alven" as designating "all the gods." Both Wanen and Alven were fertility forces and therefore this interchangeability suggests that the Wanen were in fact synonymous with the elves. It could be that both species names do reflect a difference in status, with the elves being lesser fertility gods compared to the Wanen as more distinct fertility gods. In this way, Freyr would then count as the natural ruler of the elves in Alfheim.

Chronologically, the elves could also date from an earlier time, after which they were gradually and only partially substituted by the Delusions, a more pronounced collection of individualized drives based on fertility.

145

Contemporary reimagining of a Nordic religion focusing on the Delusions is sometimes referred to as **Vanatrú**.

Delusions and their guests in a row

- Freyja
- Freyr
- Gerd
- Gullveig, When the Æsir treated her badly it caused the war between the gods
- Hœnir, an Ase hostage
- Mímir, an Ase hostage
- Kvasir
- Lýtir
- Njǫrðr
- Skaði
- Ran
- Atla

Vidar

God of Vengeance

Vidar or **Widar,** in Nordic mythology according to the Skáldskaparmál (second part of the Prose-Edda), was a silent forest god living by himself (god of silence and vengeance). He was the only son of Odin and Grid, and lived in Vidi or Landwidi ("*Landwidi*"), where everything was quiet and peaceful, with tall bushes and tall grass. According to some sources, his palace was made of leaves.

Vidar is the second strongest god. He is described as "*the silent god.*" In the LokÆsirna, he is the only one in Aegir's hall who is spared from Loki's wrath. Like Vali, he is also a vengeance god.

His destiny was to avenge his father with the Ragnarok. In fact, Odin would then be killed by the wolf Fenrir, and Vidar would kill Fenrir with his bare hands by putting his foot in the beast's mouth and splitting it open. To do this, he had a special iron-toed shoe that, according to legend, was made from the bits of leather people had cut away to keep their toes and heels free. Vidar was one of the few gods destined to survive Ragnarok.

According to the Völuspá, however, he uses his sword to kill the wolf by thrusting it straight into its heart.

After the Ragnarok, he would live in the world along with his brothers
Balder, Hodr and Vali.

Vili & Ve

Gods of Earth

Vili, in Nordic mythology, is the brother of Odin and Vé.

According to some tales, they are said to have been born from the armpit of Ymir; according to other tales, they are the sons of Borr and Bestla, which is more generally accepted. In this tale, the two giants are said to have been freed from the ice by the primordial cow.

They were the first gods, creators of the world. They killed the ice giant Ymir and from his body parts they made the world. The people Ask and Embla were made from wood pieces the three gods found on the beach.

At some point, Vili and Ve thought it was enough, while Odin was not yet satisfied. Here the separation of the gods into two "families" took place: the Æsir or *Asir*, followers of Odin, and the Vans or *Vanir*, followers of Vili and Ve.(In an Icelandic poem from the Edda, Vili is also called Honir and Ve Lodur.) After the victory of the Æsir, both families of gods (the Æsir and the Vanes) sent two of their own to the other. The Æsir were given Freya and Freyr, the Vans Mímir and Honir (or Vili). This pair initially received a warm welcome from the Vans, but they soon concluded that the exchange had not been beneficial to them. Vili was extraordinarily indecisive, expressing his opinion openly only in Mímir's absence. The Vanir got the impression that Mímir was to serve as Vili's voice and mind; therefore, they beheaded Mímir and returned his head to Asgard. Although the battle did not flare up again, a rift did grow between the Æsir and the Vanir, with the result that the Vanir's importance continued to diminish. Even in the Viking period, the distinction between Vanen and Æsir was blurred.

Vé

Vé in Nordic mythology was a vorstreus, son of Borr and of Bestla and a brother of Odin and Vili.

According to some stories, they are said to have been born from the armpit of Ymir; according to other narratives, they are the sons of Borr and Bestla, which is more generally accepted.

He and his brothers killed the ice giant Ymir, and they created the world at Ginungagap from his body parts. At one point, Vé and Vili think the world is finished, but Odin wants to go even further. Here the two families tear themselves apart: the Æsir, the followers of Odin, and the Wanen, the followers of Vé and Vili. The Teutons themselves made little distinction between the two families.

In some versions of this myth, Vé is called *Lodur* or *Lother*.

Lodur gave warmth and essence to Ask and Embla, see Voluspá.

Yggdrasil

Yggdrasil is the world tree in Nordic cosmogony. The name literally translates as "horse of Yggr," or "horse of Odin," and refers to the fierce life force that carries it and carries it everywhere.

Yggdrasil is the tree of life and knowledge, the symbol of the endlessly branched form of that which is. At the same time, it carries and connects the worlds as a world axis (axis mundi). This shows at the same time the way to the higher, the way the shaman follows to enter the realm of gods and spirits. He reaches from the underworld right through the human world to the world of gods and heroes.

Ash or yew?

Yggdrasill was often thought of in the past as a giant ash (Fraxinus Excelsior). Many scholars today agree that a mistake was once made in the interpretation of ancient writings and that the tree is most likely a yew tree (Taxus baccata). The mistake is said to have its origin in an alternative word for the yew tree in Old Norse; namely, "needle ash" (*barraskr*). In addition, ancient sources, including the Edda's, refer to a *vetgrønster vida* meaning "evergreen tree." An ash, however, loses its leaves in winter, while a yew retains its needles.

Coniferous trees were often considered sacred in the past because they never lose their greenery. The tree of life was not only a symbol from stories, but followers of nature religions also gathered around an ancient tree. Shamans fell into a trance and stories from the Eddas were told there. The yew gives off gaseous taxine on warm days, a substance that can cause hallucinations in people or even evoke a near-death experience in which the mind can temporarily leave the body. This can also be recognized in the story of Odin who, after hanging "lifeless" from the tree for nine days, received his revelation regarding the runes.

Compared to the ash, the yew has a much longer life span. The age of the Fortingall pine tree in Scotland is estimated at more than 2,000 years. In the experience of the people then, such old trees were immortal and were therefore considered sacred trees.

Etymology and meaning

Ygg means *the terrible* and *drasill* is *horse (carrying means of transportation), horsepower. Yggr* is seen as an epithet for Odin, giving it the meaning of "Odin's stallion." The horse was the favorite animal for shamans to travel between different worlds, emphasizing the connection between the nine different worlds that Yggdrasill connects.

In addition to this, the *horse* as a widespread mythological archetypal symbol, according to Carl Gustav Jung, has the double meaning of *carrying force* (which takes you everywhere) and *driving force* (natural drift). Thus, the fact that Yggdrasil is also identified with Odin's horse may indicate that this symbol denotes the **natural perpetual drift** that branches out quasi endlessly in the expression of many worlds. After all, it is also this ever-present natural urge or drive, Yggrasil, the tree of life, that survives the end of the worlds (Ragnarok) and provides a new beginning.

Moreover, according to Jung, the fact that the horse is *under* the rider would also explain its association with the natural power of the (psychic) unconscious *urges*. Indeed, Odin himself is associated with the *knowledge and wisdom* that becomes dynamic through the urges and will guide them in the right direction. This combination makes Odin a fervent warrior in word and deed.

Another meaning of *ygg* is *eternal, awesome* or *ancient/timeless*. Odin is also called yggjung (old-young)

The nine worlds that connect Yggdrasill

1. Asgaard, the world of the Ashes
2. Álfheimr, the world of light elves
3. Muspelheim, the world of fire
4. Vanaheim, the realm of fertility gods; the Vanir
5. Midgard, the world of men
6. Jötunheim, the world of the Jötuns
7. Niflheim, the realm of mists; here the dead dwelt
8. Svartalfheim (or Nidavellir), the world of black elves or dwarves
9. Helheim, the residence of the goddess Hel

Inhabitants of the tree: Mythical creatures

- High in the crest, the two-headed eagle Viðofnir watches over as a symbol of light and all-seeing clarity. He provides wind over the worlds with his wings.

- There, in some representations, there is also a waking rooster and two hawks warning the gods in case of danger. In other representations, the hawk Vedrfolnir sits on the eagle's forehead or even in his eye.
- Under the twigs the gods hold court.
- At the bottom of the roots, the primal snakes Góinn and Móinn descended from Grafvitnir (Tomb Wolf) wriggle, and the dragon Nidhogg (symbol of dark power) eats the root.
- Around the trunk live four deer with large branched antlers, Dáinn, Dvalinn, Duneyrr and Duraþrór. These live off the bark and the lower leaves and fruits.
- The squirrel Ratatoskr is messenger between the worlds, about as Hermes is to Zeus, constantly walking up and down. But he stirs up tension between the higher and the lower.
- The damage done to Yggdrasil by some of the beasts is repaired by the norns. These three women are at the roots.

Inhabitants of the tree: the gods

Most of the gods reside in Asgard, a few elsewhere as well.
See alsoGeneral overview of Germanic gods

The tree of life survives the Ragnarök

Yggdrasil is also central to the myth of the Ragnarök. When the tree of life begins to tremble, it nears the end of the world. The only two human survivors (there are some among the gods as well), Lif (life) and Lifthrasir (lust for life), can escape by hiding in the branches of Yggdrasil, where they feed on morning dew and enjoy the protection of the tree:

> *The blazing fire will not scorch them; it will not even touch them, and their food will be morning dew.*
> *Through the branches they will see a new sun ignited when the world ends and begins again*